Praise for CODE:

What happens when the rainmaker is snagged by a competitor? How can the "sales magic" be translated into a plan, a formula, that can be learned and followed with results? Elizabeth Allen's CODE process is the answer to these important questions that company owners face. Her proven process, engaging training and honest feedback help companies create a blueprint for future success.

-S.S., M.Consultants

CODE:
1. Makes us quantify the leads and how to pursue them.
2. Forces us to evaluate the job and the timing of the job. Will it fit into our schedule and how can we make it fit.
3. Makes us responsive to the clients and persistent with our follow-up.
4. Better understanding of our proprietary information
5. Pushes us to close the deal.
6. Has helped us to "know" when to say "NO" which is a good thing.
7. Prospecting: The importance of being seen in the community and the value of visibility.

-N.N., V.P. Secretary Treasurer, N. Construction

It's been over three years since I've completed the CODE Training Program for business development. This program has shaped the way I approach sales and given our organization a clear process for business development activities. CODE has positively impacted my ability to sell by providing motivation, accountability, and useful sales tools. Personally, I use many of the CODE lessons and tools as part of my everyday work habits. The 8 Questions That MUST be Answered for Each Prospect is a very effective process for qualifying leads. This methodology puts me in charge of the conversation with a prospect, and drives the flow of many initial meetings. Working with Elizabeth

Allen as a sales coach truly accelerated my learning curve of the CODE process and increased my motivation to sell. She has what it takes to kick start entry level staff as well as fine tune executive level talent. I would recommend CODE to those who want to sell without any hesitation.

-M. D., Community Relations Director, C.Construction

The adoption of the CODE process has truly revolutionized how the sales team looks at not only their job tasks, but the job of selling as a whole. The intrinsic value that CODE helps bring to the confidence level of a sales person has been transforming. As the sales manager for three offices, I have seen the transformation of sales people in a very short time. The results to the bottom line are not yet recognized, but at this stage, the process has been worth the investment. CODE is a simple platform in which to guide the sales process and sales team members in an easy and consistent format. This consistency is lacking in many sales organizations today. CODE helps not only recognize the short comings but how to combat them. From a coaching standpoint, CODE has provided a personal side benefit I did not expect. For the first time in my 15 year career as a sales manager in some shape or form, I truly have the confidence to KNOW what to do next as a sales manager. Like many others, I am the result of an excellent sales person being put in management to train others to do what I do well. CODE has not only shown the weaknesses of our sales team, but helped define the strengths of our team and the process in which our company will negate or eliminate the weaknesses. I look forward to a long and prosperous sales cycle of increased growth for many years to come.

-S.L., Vice President, A.S. Design

THE CONTRACTOR'S CODE

FOR MARKETING & SALES

BY

ELIZABETH ALLEN

Table of Contents

Foreword

Why I love this book

by
Michael E. Gerber
Author of _The E-Myth_

Yes, I do love this book. In fact, I wish I had written it. I believe you're going to love it too, for exactly the same reasons that I do.

And that's because in this book Elizabeth Allen has struck the impossible chord...a resonant response to a universal problem in all companies...how to standardize the _unstandardizable_...how to turnkey the seemingly too sophisticated process through which any company can with great predictability identify its most important prospects, convert them into champions, and deliver its promise to them with certainty and conviction no matter who in the company is accountable for the process. Provided, of course, that they, the ones accountable, have learned, internalized, integrated and implemented in their practice what Elizabeth calls so resolutely, and, I might say, religiously, "The CODE®."

Yes, Elizabeth Allen's "CODE" is a religion of sorts for those who have internalized it. A religion, because The CODE has this uncanny way of signifying the truth.

Once you read The CODE, and apply it to your company, you will immediately see why your client acquisition capability up to this point in time – the time you are confronted with The CODE -- leaves so much to be desired.

And that's because without The CODE there is no certainty in what you do.
Without The CODE, there is no replicable method for producing consistent, significantly above average results in your company.

Without The CODE. there is no objective measure for quantifying client acquisition activities across your sales organization, let alone in accounting, or operations, or any other function within your organization which struggles with the question: what can we depend upon today, tomorrow, or next month?

The CODE answers that question, and many more just like it, with the clarity of a ringing bell.

So, thank you Elizabeth Allen for introducing me to The CODE and The CODE to your readers.

I know it will become exactly that kind of book that stays with us for years and years ahead. A brilliant classic. A stunning epiphany. A profoundly original contribution to the world of work.

Michael E. Gerber
Author of ***Awakening The Entrepreneur Within***
and ***The E-Myth***, Carlsbad, California, 2007

An Introduction.

This book is dedicated to all the Tom, Dick and Harrys.

Sound familiar?
It's a typical day at Acme General Contractors (insert Architects or Engineers, if appropriate). At this company, there are three key salesmen: Tom Acme, the president; Dick Acme, his brother; and Harry – an estimator in operations who helps with managing sales leads.

I'm sure you can guess the background, but let's take a moment to fill in the blanks:

Tom and Dick are third-generation company leaders; their grandfather, who had founded the company, had passed it to their father, and their father had passed it on to them. They maintain good community standing by providing sound leadership and have longstanding memberships on every board and community service program that they can squeeze into their busy schedules. Often at the sacrifice of personal and family time, the brothers have promoted the business and have "networked like crazy" to promote it. Harry helps with sales and serves primarily as an estimator in operations, but does his best to support Tom and Dick's efforts. These are the issues that each member of the team faces:

Tom is the rainmaker, president and closer. All sales efforts really come down to his ability to generate leads, manage the relationships, run the sales process and close the deals. It's a lot of work, and at this point, he's getting tired. *Really tired.* At night he wakes up afraid of the day he exits the company, as there is nothing he can depend on should something happen to him personally. He has no "plan B" outside of his brother or possibly hiring another senior level business development person. *But that option presents challenges, too.*

If he finds an excellent sales person, the problem still remains that the person can leave at any given time, taking his contacts with him -- maybe even going to a competitor! What are the options? Tom isn't a sales trainer, he doesn't know how to coach his people in developing critical sales skills, and he is even more concerned when reviewing the options associated with recent graduates.

Tom's experience has lead him to believe that the new hires prioritize time off and simply refuse to put in the required after-hours to effectively network. This is unnerving when he considers what it took to get him to the required level of community involvement that it takes to be truly "in the know" about upcoming work.

And then there's the cycles of the industry, feast or famine, boom or bust....He is continually asking, how do you get ahead and keep a profitable backlog full? The cycles are brutal, and keeping the pipeline full is very tough, even for the seasoned prospector.

Really, he wonders ...what can I do?

Dick, Tom's brother and vice-president of operations, also feels the pain. He tries to help with generating leads and offers input on marketing efforts, but he really isn't sure how the marketing plan and budget should work together to support sales. There is absolutely no clear return on investment as it relates to the marketing dollars spent and the quality of leads generated.

He wishes there was a list they could buy that would identify people who would be buying or building new buildings. *If they only knew where to advertise or how to market more effectively, maybe then they could get ahead of the competition.* Right now, Dick worries that when a potential customer evaluates his firm, there really is little tangible difference between his company and other competitors.

He worries everyone tells the "quality" story, and that without an intimate knowledge of the marketplace, it's difficult for the customer to distinguish one company from another. *He sees little differentiation amongst companies, and it seems like the industry in general is being commoditized.*

All too often things come down purely to price, because, let's face it, sometimes you just need the work. Like everyone, he struggles to maintain focus on the long sales cycles, he is tired of being called for bids, feels often at the mercy of architects, and struggles to keep the customer pipeline full with legitimate leads. He wishes there was a more organized approach to the market that would drive tangible results. Considering that every other aspect of the business, from project management to accounting to safety has a process, why doesn't business development and sales have a process? As far as he can tell, it's flipping voodoo.

Harry, the chief estimator, is very tired. As the estimating department leader, he feels the impact of being "called for bids" at the ground level. When a call from a prospect comes in, and it's negotiated or design build work, frequently he finds that "they simply want a bid for the work being proposed." The lead says "negotiated or design build," but in reality it plays out to be "ballpark short-list bid."

Frequently the lead is already working with an architect; the design work is in progress, and now the architect has suggested that they "request bids" from general contractors. Externally, there is little direct contact with the buyer, diminished input on the design and little influence on how to create cost-saving efficiencies. In the end, it all too often comes down to price -- which is *extremely frustrating*.

Internally, Harry sees that estimating is overworked and is frustrated with the number of hours spent on detailed proposals that are simply being shopped, or worse, simply being reviewed for subcontractor information.

When a lead comes in and it lands on his desk, he struggles to qualify the lead. Where is the prospect in the decision-making process? What opportunities do we have to take the emphasis off of price? To narrow the competitive field? To spend quality time with the decision-maker? He never would say it, but at times he thinks that lead management seems to run like a game of "who has the business card?"

Then there's the issue of where we go to even find qualified leads. Harry wants to help identify prospects, but typically by the time he knows about the lead, so does the competition. By the time he reads about the new development, expansion or business in town, it's public knowledge. Harry's unsure what to do and simply wants to succeed.

He's just not sure how "success" is defined... and worries increasingly that management doesn't have an answer to the question either.

And then there may be on the team ...
"The marketer, bird dog, or director of business development"
Depending on the size of the company and the commitment to growth, this role may or may not exist. If it does, you

might have been with this team a few years – just out of college or an intern -- or many years, working as the marketing director or VP of business development.

Should you be of senior level experience, the company naturally looks to you for the marketing plan. But, let's face it, *your real challenge is how to effectively implement the plan*, which is supposed to drive "branding" and lead-generation efforts. You may find that the company rallies around the battle cry for a strategic marketing plan, but then balks when you suggest monitoring true day-to-day sales team activities.

Since the principal (or "rainmaker") essentially owns prospect generation, how do you effectively influence his day-to-day sales and lead generation activities? Isn't it the "job of marketing" to help generate and qualify leads? You worry that although the concept of the marketing plan is theoretically sound, the bridge to driving day-to-day sales performance and team accountability isn't.

You have to carefully choose your battles, and unless the principal comes to the awareness on his own that "there's a problem" with the way we as a company are doing things...things can't effectively be changed.

Culturally, any change must originate from him. *So what do you do?* Where do you start? You are tired of the "let's-sponsor-the-golf-tournament strategy," as you have a hard time quantifying return on investment, and with a very limited budget, you really wish there was a more cost-effective way to conduct this whole "branding" effort you're responsible for.

In your quiet moments, you consider the challenge of branding "Acme Brothers Construction Company" to be about as interesting as branding "John Doe Builders." *How can you create a lingering memorable impression when the name of the company is the last name of the principals?* The last time the company redesigned the logo was in 1979 when somebody's cousin took an art course, and every item in the company – from letterhead to the trucks -- has a different version of the same outdated art. There is little to no consistency.

So how do you even begin to launch into the discussion that it's time to get serious about the image of the company when you really don't know what you'd do even if you did have the budget?

Are you on this team? Are you struggling with these or similar issues?

Perhaps your situation or firm is slightly different, but I suspect you are reading this because you can relate to the pain felt by this team.

These issues make the industry's financial cycles terribly painful for contractors, architects and engineers. These are the things that trouble and frustrate business development teams. They undermine the exit or succession strategy for a family-owned business. These are the things that almost all companies in the industry struggle with, and frequently they go unaddressed until the situation becomes critical. Your company goes from one job to the next in good times, until one day there's just no more jobs to go to.

No matter where your firm falls on the food chain in the building or contracting industry, everyone in the industry can relate to these issues as they engage in the same "relationship-driven" sales process.

If you are an executive leader, business development manager, new sales trainee or even a construction industry intern, it's time to reconsider the approach to making sales and business development happen. Anyone pursuing business development or marketing in the industry needs to explore a *very fresh perspective* on a definitive sales process.

Why? Because this issue of how you really go about and effectively engage with business development is of *extreme interest* to those in the industry. Currently, there's little training available, there are few management tools, and if you find yourself in the role of leading business development, everyone wants to add their two cents to the direction of the strategic plan.

It's fair to say that everyone in the industry really does want to talk about the issue, hash out the details and compare notes -- but because it's so competitive, there's an industry wide code of silence. Sitting in a crowd of peer group companies, it's so quiet the silence can be deafening. Evidence of this is everywhere.

The Vow of Silence

I recently attended a "business development forum" sponsored by a local chapter of the Society of Professional Marketing Services (SMPS). The focus of the talk was how to conduct business development; it was led by a great director of business development for a local general contractor. The promotional flier for the event promised a 20-minute Q&A forum where "no question is off limits." *(Hmmm...)*

The anticipated attendance was strong as the program had been offered before, but the *actual* attendance was nearly standing room only. Because it had been promoted by the local DBIA chapter (Design Build Institute of America), at the last moment, streams of general contractor business development folks streamed in the door.

9

My guest, when scanning the faces around the room, could take a roll call of all his regional competitors. He was shocked all of these people had taken time out of their day in the hopes of finding a magic bullet. I had invited him so that we could review another valid perspective on the issue. And I'll be first to say that the presentation was good, as it provided some strong suggestions on where to spend time conducting business development – highlighting attitudes and behaviors that are important to remember.

But the presentation ended there.
It didn't provide specific steps or tools that you could implement today to align your business development efforts up to best-practice caliber. In general, it was a collection of ideas and observations about the business development attitude. It was a good presentation, and I sensed people left with a few new ideas, but perhaps not the solid action plan that they were looking for. *Why not?*

Let's address a painful truth about the construction industry as a whole.

The demand for a sales and marketing solution is very strong...but so is the competition among the players. Silence is the elephant in the room that, when push comes to shove, nobody can afford to breach.

So what's to give? No one wants to reveal a compelling sales strategy in very competitive markets. *And what market isn't competitive?* If you find the magic bullet to making your marketing and sales strategy sing like a canary, you are no more going to go tell your competition than the man in the moon. *You'd rather eat staples. I realize this.* However, I want to remind you that much like the process your company goes through to assure safety – the process that you engage with to actually build a building –

you also really need a process for sales. You know how to build buildings, and to do it, you follow a clear process. Step by step, you prepare, plan and execute to produce a finished product. *It is very predictable.* I want to assure you that the same principle is true for sales.

The purpose of this book is to provide to you the exact steps your team should follow so that you can create a predictable customer pipeline, a process that will help you to counter the pain of the "hard bid" world you live in. This process will provide you confidence to offset the die-hard reality of the commodity mindset indeed that *cripples* this industry.

There is an absolute step-by-step process. You simply need to know what to do as well as the rules and roles that are critical in order to manage the expectations of the prospect at every stage in the game. After many years of researching this subject, I am pleased to assure you that you can use the *very* limited internal resources that you have to develop a truly "predictable customer pipeline." Aren't you pleased to know that you have control over this issue?

So let's break the silence and get real with one another. (As a consultant, if I had the privilege of sitting across from you at this moment, I'd carefully study your posture and quietly ask you the following questions)...

Really, where are you with your business? How satisfied are you, as a business owner? Has a lack of profitable backlog or few qualified prospects deeply concerned you? Are you tired of being the only rainmaker? Are you tired of competing on price alone? Or, has your firm hit a sales and revenue plateau that seemingly can't be broken? Does your team have great ideas *but poor execution*? Perhaps your team is looking for a marketing or sales solution to a problem that seems so darn vast that it's hard to define.

If so, you need to ask yourself if you are willing to change the way you do things to change the position you are in.

This is a serious question, and one that deserves very careful consideration before you answer. I want to draw your attention to the analogy of sustained weight loss. It may sound strange, but achieving long-term weight loss is actually *very similar* to executing a strong sales process.

How do you lose weight? Assuming no serious medical problems, we all know the answer to sustained weight loss is actually very simple: eat right and exercise. Eat less and move more. But how hard is it in this day and age to simply "eat right and exercise?" If you ask the one in three adults in the U.S. who struggle with their weight, they'll tell you it's *very* hard. It is very difficult to change deeply entrenched habits, so you really have to want to change or *recognize that change is seriously required* for there to be even a "possibility" of sustained change.

In a similar way, following a very specific sales program can be difficult. *Why?* Because the bottom line is that it will require you to change the way you think and act on some fundamental level.

Think about it this way. If you were to swim to the middle of a moving stream, treading water to maintain your perceived target, it would nearly be impossible to stay in the same place. You would constantly be moving forward or backward.

The same principle is true in sales. You are always moving forward or backward, but *rarely,* if ever, staying in the exact same place.

12

So where is your team? Moving forward or backward?

A new approach is somewhat easy in the beginning because it's novel. It's the "flavor of the day." (For the first two weeks, those protein cookies actually taste good.) However, sustaining long-term cultural change requires the dedicated focus of the team once past the implementation phase.

Are you willing to consider "changing your approach" to the market? *Is your team?*

One of the challenges I face as a consulting coach is to get you to simply *admit* that you could do things better, that there is enough "pain" in your company or business development team that it is time to truly try something new. As the book *Good to Great* states very clearly, the enemy to becoming a great company is simply to be satisfied that things are "good enough." So be brutally honest with yourself. **Are things to a point where you are really willing to change, or are things "good enough?"**

What kind of changes are we talking about? Let's start with the tough one: accountability. *If you lead a company, the process will require you to lead by example. Did I hear an "Ouch?"* If you work on a team, this approach to organizing sales efforts will require you to be accountable. In a typical midsized company where most people on the sales force are accustomed to "doing their own thing" and not really following a process, this really can be a tough issue to address.

Will the culture at your company support accountability? Are you as a leader willing to become accountable? Can you as a leader demonstrate enough commitment to change that your team will avoid the "flavor-of-the-day" sentiment that *this too shall pass*?

In certain instances, managers of teams I've coached wanted their teams to become accountable, but wished to avoid accountability at the leadership level. This is a dangerous double standard; when it's exposed to a formalized process, all those participating conclude that there is a lack of committed leadership.

This has been especially evident when the team is required to create short-term "to-do" lists, and week after week, the leaders of the team shirk the responsibility, simply explaining that they don't have the time, which translates to all involved that it's not a priority. I've often seen this happen, which is why I bring it to your attention. *So be careful for what you wish for!* Many marketers and business development teams complain that it's impossible to track return on investment when it comes to marketing and sales without an elaborate and technology-driven system... but I disagree.

Through simple reporting and documentation, it is possible to determine return on investment. **Are you ready to exceed your expectations with regards to performance?** *Are you willing to try new sales tactics that may challenge you to expand your communication skills?*

When considering the two human motivators -- pleasure and pain – I almost hate to say it, but serious pain tends to be the primary motivator that ensures long-term and sustainable change.

The good news and bad news: Is your team in "positive" pain? Is your pain defined by the desire to take market share that right now is out of reach? Do you desire to grow your company to the next phase of revenue growth, and does it frustrate you that you don't know how? If so, you must ask yourself if you are willing to lead by example.

Only companies that are willing to change and recognize the need to change at the leadership level actually have what it takes to achieve and sustain it. (Please stop and *really think* about that last statement.)

Is your team facing a "negative" kind of pain?
Negative pain is *easy* to describe. It's the pain that company leaders face when they realize that if work doesn't materialize, layoffs or other tough decisions are imminent. Negative pain can assume the form of extreme frustration among the executive leaders when there is no clear indication of *what to do* on a day-to-day basis to identify new prospects. Negative pain can be what frustrates employees, causes lack of focus or performance among the sales team, or in worst case, is the motive for layoffs or other company-altering decisions.

Which brings us again to the critical point: change has to be initiated from the top down in organizations. Do you believe that things on some level need to change? That things need to be improved? That the pain, whether positive or negative, can be overcome?

What you believe is important...but so is your definition of "success."

When conducting the national test pilot for the program I've developed called CODE, I was able to learn from various companies the many definitions and viewpoints surrounding program success. For one firm, a week after training, the principal of the company called me to cancel the first progress meeting.

When I asked why, he replied that in obtaining the CODE training materials and book, he had (in his mind) achieved success. He defined success as "a book he could ask others to read" so that they would "know what to do" when he hired them. His definition stopped at the point of having training for new hires. It had absolutely *nothing* to do with implementing and actually running the program.

Fortunately, other companies I've coached have defined success in more tangible terms. Here's a partial list of definitions for success that I've encountered. As you review these, ask yourself how your team would define success. What would constitute a "win" for the team and a new sales approach? Here are common ways I've seen companies define success.

Definitions of Success

Use the following statements to mentally end the question, "I define success with a sales process as having. . ."

A "scorecard" with which to really evaluate our progress toward defined new

business goals, bridging the gap between our business development plan and our day- to-day performance.

A process that will help us close more deals or be more selective about the deals we choose to pursue, getting us out of a "feast or famine" mentality.

A method to take control of interacting with decision-makers, a set of tools and philosophies that will teach us to add value to our services, differentiating us from aggressive competitors and industry commoditization.

Peace of mind about a full pipeline and knowing that the team understands its role in supporting "rainmaking" efforts.

A way to manage the team members, their expectations and productivity in such a way so that we as a company can retain and reward our best talent.

An exit strategy. I need a program to profitably sustain growth for the company and transition key skills so that sales are not dependent on any one person everything can't come down to one or two key people.

If these are your definitions of success, this program was created to specifically address these issues. So now if I were to share with you the greatest solution, it will lose its strength at the point of impact if leadership doesn't hold the team accountable and drive the plan for implementation.

Will you work with me? I need a commitment... *but perhaps more importantly, your team will require it.* In the following chapters, I will outline a turnkey program -- generated from the working experiences of companies just like yours – that will finally and forever take the mystery out of how your strategic marketing plan should integrate against the day-to-day activities of your sales team.

Now I challenge you to open your mind to a new and very simple version of sales and marketing. In the upcoming chapters, I will introduce to you a new way to think about lead generation, prospecting efforts, marketing and the sales process. Hopefully in reviewing the detail, you'll be surprised with its simplicity.

Too often, consultants have worked with the indirect goal of making complicated what should be a very simple process. Unfortunately, it's in their best interest to keep you second guessing and attending motivational seminars. So in the next few chapters I pledge to cut the mystery out of marketing and business development voodoo. No "consultant" speak, only the truth about what works and why, in the most straightforward method that I can deliver it.

Intrigued? This book will outline a simple yet exact process that you need to overcome your sales issues. Specifically, I'll address:

How to market your firm in the most cost-effective manner possible to build an effective and compelling brand image.

How to organize your prospecting efforts so that you can "predictably fill the

prospect pipeline"- no more guessing when it comes to assessing where someone is in the sales process or wondering "what the next step should be."

How to and where to find prospects when they don't easily identify themselves; how you can get a step ahead of everyone else so that you can identify and impact prospects before they even realize that they are prospects.

How to effectively position your company from the customer's perspective so

that, from the first contact forward, you have a distinct advantage over the competition.

How to qualify and categorize each lead, so that you don't invest valuable internal resources on leads that aren't going anywhere.

The importance of setting an agenda for each point of contact with a prospect so that each contact is meaningful.

Methods to stay focused and motivated when you are in a very long sales process, one that can take anywhere from 18 to 24 months.

How to address clearly and with purpose the issues of price, proprietary solutions and competition so that you control and manage the expectations of the prospect through a series of disclosures that puts you in the driver's seat throughout your sales effort.

Use of communication techniques designed to take the emphasis off of price. You will be able to subtly make the prospect aware of all the things that they don't know that can seriously hurt them if they make decisions simply by price.

Sound good?

Let's begin filling your company's pipeline with profitable prospects.

Chapter One

The Story Behind the Story...
Necessity Truly is the Mother of Invention.

The story I introduced to you is fictional, but it is a compilation of true events and people that I have encountered many times in working with companies in the architectural, engineering, and construction industries. I began to seriously study this industry when I was called in by a $15 million construction company president struggling with all the issues I've mentioned.

He said to me, "Elizabeth, you are in advertising. You write marketing plans and seem to understand the sales process. Find me a list of people who will build buildings in the near future. Help me find them and effectively market to them...and we'll be successful at growing our top-line revenue. Surely this list is out there. We can't seem to find it, but maybe you can."

What a clear challenge and a specific mission. I liked it. Initially, I believed as he did that surely this list was "out there" and maybe direct mail or highly targeted communications could help drive a campaign that could lead to greater top-line revenue growth. For goodness sake, we live in a digital age with almost *anything* at our fingertips. This really couldn't be that hard.

Discovering the Brutal Truth About "the Invisible Prospect"

But ah, after much research I discovered it was harder than it seemed. Much harder. Having worked in the advertising industry for years and being familiar with direct marketing methods, I began the search for "the list." And yes, list brokers (or Co-Star) could produce tentative lists based on certain criteria, but none I had too much confidence in.

You see, my client had already tried direct mail efforts to identify the businesses that they thought might be expanding, building or renovating, but with very little, *if any,* success. My client had sent out information to companies that might be building in the future and found that *unless it was requested information,* the return on the effort was nominal at best. They would send information out and unless it was asked for, *nobody* reading the mail would step up and say, "Why yes, I'll be building in the next year or so, I'll call you." Or better yet, "please call us."

Nope, nobody wanted to step up and identify themselves. Yet we knew businesses were exploring options and needed help. *Why wouldn't they respond?*

After more investigation, there were still more questions than answers. We knew that people in the market were at all phases of exploring options with building, but we discovered that by the time that they realized and identified themselves as "prospects," typically all my client's competitors knew it too. In the earliest stages of awareness, the prospect typically had been talking to their bankers and attorneys...and were referred to my client's competitors. *Not good.*

Now you can't influence everyone in this food chain, but it sure seemed reasonable to assume that with focused efforts, you could do something to reach the decision-maker in a timely fashion.

This seemed like a simple assumption, but the market had put this to test against the hard truth that the prospect "wasn't mentally in the market" to gather information or identify themselves as prospects until they were almost ready to build, buy or relocate.

This is a big darn problem for contractors because time is the critical component when establishing a relationship, creating credibility and educating the client on your approach to creating value for them.

Sadly, time is not on your side...

Once the light comes on and the prospect begins to review vendors, timing is not on the contractor's side, as it becomes increasingly difficult to establish a relationship or endear the value of your brand to them. It's all about relationships.

As you know, the prospect typically seeks a referral (from his financer or business advisor who has a stake in the deal) and lands in the lap of key competitors. Should they choose to shop around, by the time you find out or are approached to "put together a bid," it almost always comes down to price. At best, you are simply responding and hoping for a break.

My client was really tired of this and wanted to be proactive.

Why be proactive?

Easy. When you have no time to establish a relationship with the client it always comes down to price -- and you've been commoditized. Other companies and players "own the
relationship with the client"...and we all know how the story ends.

Let me provide to you an intuitive, consumer-based illustration of this principle that will shock you. Have you ever noticed that there are *always* car sales and mattress sales going on at any given time? *I mean, any day of the week, any month of the year -- there's always some company out there on radio and TV advertising like crazy to sell you a car or mattress.* Why is this? I was in advertising for years and always was humorously amused at the near stupidity of the situation. "It's an overstock sale, inventory clearance...my dog's got a flea sale"....and on and on it goes. *It literally never stops.*

There's always a sale going. Why?

Surely they can't be as pathetic as they would seem with inventory management.

The truth? These companies constantly advertise because one day, your Chevy will die on the freeway for the umpteenth time, and you'll *suddenly* be in the market for a new car. You'll have "had it" with that car. Or one day, you wake up, look down and decide that the overly familiar neck ache is *reason enough* to retire the mattress from hell.

Do you get my point? You go from *not* being really in the market – or *tuning out* the noise -- until one day *out of the blue* you suddenly find yourself in enough "pain" to take action or seek informational options. You aren't a prospect until *out of the clear blue sky* the light comes on and suddenly – *why yes, you are indeed a prospect.*

And the advertiser that gets to you first, the brand that peaks your interest, has a great shot at your business.

This same exact phenomena is true in most industries. A buyer of services "suddenly appears" and you get a call out of the blue. *And depending on where she is at in her* *awareness of her need, you can anticipate exactly what will happen.*

What's the drill?

You are asked to "bid" by another services provider, or the client may want multiple estimates within several proposals, and it's not clear to you *at all* what the client really wants or how they'll make the decision, because you've had little time to establish communications and expectations with the decision-maker. This reality is *equally true* for architects and engineers.

This is a very difficult reality, and classic advertising and marketing isn't a solution because decisions are relationship-driven at the most executive level in businesses. Although the promise of maintaining a memorable brand is enticing and sounds like a silver bullet solution, very few firms have the dollars or savvy to properly place and maintain the brand through extensive advertising, promotions or PR efforts.

In simplest terms, most contractors, architects or engineering firms can't afford the true financial commitment that is required to sustain a memorable brand in the marketplace. Let's look at another fact. Most companies have names like Smith & Sons or ANCB Builders, so creating a memorable "brand" around a last name or acronym begins to take on a challenge of ominous proportions. Face it, you simply don't have the budget of Orville Redenbacher.

So what are the options? *What gives?*

How do you identify and manage prospects through such a strange and long sales cycle? Anyone familiar with the industry knows that from start to finish of the sales cycle, it can easily be as long as 18 to 24 months; that's a *long time* to stay focused by any standard. On the most basic level we asked, "Where do you go and how do you begin to find qualified leads when they won't identify themselves?"

To my client, the challenge was clear and the solution was not. We both asked:

? How do you find a prospect and make meaningful contact with him before he even *realizes* that he is a prospect?

? How do you identify the prospect so you can ask the important questions to truly qualify her before you spend valuable internal resources on estimating? How can you make the process seamless?

? How do you take all the steps necessary to ensure your best shot at business development while utilizing a consistent process designed to help you reliably predict the likelihood to close the new opportunities you've identified?

? What role can each member of the team play so that it is clear to all exactly what to do and how to do it? What should update reports and meetings look like?

Studying the Obvious
How you do... Why you do... What you do, every day...whether you recognize it or not. When faced with these questions, my first response was to dig in and look carefully at what had contributed to the success of the organization to date. Launched in the mid-'70s, my client's company had grown to a comfortable stage of "mid-market" revenue growth. They were by all definitions "successful" in what they were doing, they just wanted to be *more* successful. They had done so many things right; they were in "positive pain." What I wanted to study were the intuitive processes that supported specifically *how* they

were doing things so that we could improve the focus of these activities and make the likelihood of success stronger.

With this as my mission, I began to study how leads were generated, processed and closed among the key three members of the sales team. I thought if I could simply help them understand what they are doing naturally, then maybe I could help them identify the areas to improve. I believe sincerely in the old adage, if you can't measure it, it can't be improved (remember the weight loss analogy?). This is so very true in sales.

I knew from my years of working with other clients that if you don't know where you are at in a clear process, with some type of mechanism to gauge your progress, making true, lasting change becomes very difficult. At best, you can maintain status quo; this perhaps best summarizes my client's status. They had engaged with some programs to better understand sales behaviors, but they had no formal sales process.

They also felt there was a disconnect between the advertising dollars spent, their marketing strategy and their sales efforts. They desired a program to cost effectively tie everything together. In marketing terms, they were looking for full integration between marketing and sales. This was at the heart of their challenge or "positive pain."

Like most small- to mid-sized businesses, they tended to treat marketing and sales as distinct disciplines, with little strategic or direct connectivity. The goals of my efforts were to definitively align all marketing, sales and advertising efforts so that, for once, all outcomes were synchronized to produce measurable results.

This had to be accomplished utilizing the skills inherent to the organization, with limited outside consulting help or new hires. Although I was an accessible resource, for the long-term success of this newly aligned approach, the program had to prove to be self-sustaining. So this became another aspect of the goal.

The Team
Let's take a moment to talk about the client's team. They simply had the rainmaker, his brother (the construction division president) and a former intern who worked with them under the title of marketing coordinator. *Sound familiar?*

In their minds, the demon that they struggled with was commonly referred to as a "marketing" problem, because they felt it was the responsibility of the marketer to help identify and focus efforts that would generate qualified leads (defined as negotiated or design build work).

After examination, on a certain level it was a marketing problem in that their brand was outdated and did need some polishing. Perhaps more importantly though, they had a significant lead generation or sales problem.

They lacked the tools, clearly defined roles and corresponding responsibilities to truly scale and maximize their efforts.

Leveraging "The Human Brand"
Marketing and advertising consultants are going to want to shoot me for this next statement, but advertising or branding efforts alone are not the solutions to the problem the construction industry faces. *It is a much more complex problem.* Think about it. The biggest construction players in the nation don't spend a lot on advertising.

They join community boards, contribute donations to high-profile charities and executive golf tournaments and put as many people into the commercial market as possible to create the face of a "human brand." This results in generating, maintaining and leveraging executive-level relationships from which they glean information, which leads to sales opportunities. With most of the effort being PR-related and "networking"-based, how is it that certain companies still have such a *tangible presence and noteworthy brand* in key markets?

Before I answer that question, stop and *really* think about it.

The answer is both obvious and painfully simple. The major contractor companies that dominate in key markets tend to have CREWS and CRAINS and JOBSITES virtually everywhere.

They've achieved a visual market momentum that's difficult to deny by appearing to be everywhere with signs and logos supporting their brand.

Once they hit a point of visual critical mass, every job they are on then supports their "human branding" PR effort in the most aggressive way possible.

In a reflective moment, my client asked, "How can mid-market companies take on the titans of the construction industry? How can we out-maneuver the giants who are on every committee and board in town? How do you fight fair with competitors who have war chests as big as Dallas?" *How could my client truly take on Goliath?*

This quandary was fueling the problem my client was wrestling with. Convinced that I loved the sheer challenge of out-marketing companies with much deeper pockets, I decided I needed to dig in and try to identify a solution.

I asked my great client, "If I defined, improved and documented their best efforts in the way they conducted sales, could I have the rights to share it with the industry?" *Yes, they* would allow me that privilege.

In an effort to pioneer best practices and bring them to the industry, this *extraordinary leader broke the code of silence*, and you have him to thank. This client was then even *kind enough* to introduce me to other trusted peers in the industry so we could determine if what they were doing, when compared with a group of similar high growth, national contractors, would constitute "best practice" in the industry.

And amazingly, what my client was doing *was* identified as best practice in the group.

The chapters that follow are the outcome of what I've learned and what happened. And it's a story with a happy ending, as my client was able to **double** its top-line revenue within one year of implementation.

In an effort to really summarize the activities you do in each phase of the sales process, you'll find here a checklist of helpful CODE tips to get started. It's followed by discussion questions and a quick self-quiz so you can test what you've learned. Each chapter features this section at the end to help you jump into the process.

Now – if you're ready to make changes and to commit to doing things differently – join me on this journey of discovery, trial and error.

Chapter Two

Your Sales Team Is Organized,
It Just May Not Be Obvious

Construction companies are notoriously casual. They typically don't have a formal organization chart for the company, they usually have loosely defined team roles as it relates to sales... and as a bonus, they even dress casually most of the time. There are some advantages to this, as it allows for flexibility and creativity.

However, in a sales or business development environment, it can be frustrating- who is supposed to do what? What is each person really responsible for? Even though my client had no official sales titles, they did operate according to unspoken rules that paralleled their skill sets. Here is a summary of what I found when I examined the composition of their sales team. *As I describe these people, ask yourself, "Who on my team plays these roles or has these skills?"*

Three Critical Roles Required for Sales

The Closer:
At the helm, leading almost all sales efforts, is the President and official Rainmaker. He is the guy (or gal) visually associated with the company- the face that locally everyone knows. He is on the community boards, participates in community events and is generally the visionary responsible for making things happen in the area of sales. He landed this role because, let's face it, he founded (or in some cases inherited) the company. He is where the "buck stops"... but is also literally where most of the new project bucks start.

He not only identifies deals (generates leads), but also had the technical and negotiating skill sets to close the deals. He is "The Closer" who embodies all essential skills necessary to run the show and manage every aspect of customer relations. Typically the owner of the company has mastered all of the issues associated with every aspect of selling, so it comes *naturally* to them. They also have the years of building experience to address almost any technical concern that might come up (they embody the skills of the Technical Expert).

Whether they consciously realize it or not, they tend to sell "all the time" with enthusiasm to every contact they meet- because they live, eat and breathe the joy of new sales and business ownership. **They are entrepreneurs in every sense of the word**. They've invested in and literally built the communities in which they live- so they have no problem telling with pride the story to prospects of what the company is, why it's special, and what they can do. The Closers literally love telling the story of the company, and as entrepreneurial leaders, they do it with a natural credibility that creates spark and interest.

Although they have a tendency to want to review almost every lead the company has, they *usually cannot possibly touch each lead due to the sheer volume*. This said, they do get involved with leads that are considered very hot, as they tend to have the skills to rapidly assess the situation and determine how it should be pursued. Their ability to sense the *intent* of the prospect tends to be quite honed, and they tend to know when "someone is simply fishing for a price" with little or no intention of moving forward.

They naturally know how to establish rapport, and they ask with *sensitivity and timing* key financial qualifier questions. Due to the fact they are engrossed in their communities, their networks of contacts tend to generate many "leads" that require further qualification. Since they tend to be heavily involved in operations as well, the time that they invest in company marketing is *quite valuable.* They tend to place themselves in the center of new deals; sometimes they have a tough time *relinquishing control* over the prospect in an effort to transfer the lead to other members of the team. Since they have so much at stake, they tend to rightfully act very "hands on."

The Technical Expert:
The second typical player on the sales team has many technical skills and operational responsibilities. Perhaps they come from project management, operations or estimating. They tend to participate strongly in lead management in an effort to support the Closer. Their technical experience makes them the individual to answer tough technical questions, and their years in the industry tend to make them confident in making presentations to prospects. In architectural firms, they are most likely the architects or key technical talent. Or in engineering firms-they may be project managers.

Their time is very valuable, and they really don't like to attend sales meetings where the prospect is unqualified. When this happens they perceive it to be a big waste of their time, as they tend to directly contribute to the companies growth through the almighty "billable hours". They are great management people with strong technical knowledge and operational skills, but they tend to have less charisma and outgoing communication capabilities than their counterparts, the Intern, New Sales Guy, Marketing Coordinator or Bird Dog.

The Prospector:
(AKA "The Intern, Sales Guy, Marketing Coordinator or Bird Dog")

32

In a contracting company this person's title can be anything from Marketing Director to New Business Development Manager to Sales Manager or Administrative Intern. The difference in title comes largely from the number of years they've been in the industry. If they are at entry level, they may be the Marketing Administrator or Sales Coordinator. If they are truly seasoned, they may be the VP of Sales and Business Development. Either way, this person has specific personality traits that make them an integral part of the marketing, sales and prospecting efforts.

Who is this person? If they were hired to be in sales or business development, they will be outgoing, charismatic, communicative and focused on building personal relationships. If they were hired as marketers or graphic design/administrative support, they will tend to be more analytical, process-driven or administration-oriented in their job function.

As a rule, marketers tend to be outgoing, communicative and competitive. They are detail-minded and like to play a supporting role in the sales efforts. At most firms if they are an entry-level hire, they are responsible for assembling proposals and brochure packets, website updates and coordination of outside advertising activities.

Often as an entry-level hire, they lack the industry or technical knowledge or confidence to aggressively support outbound prospecting efforts associated with sales. This said, whether they like it or not, or feel comfortable or not, oftentimes they are called to assist on sales calls with lead management, which can make them feel awkward, unqualified or unprepared.

Again, depending on their years in the industry and comfort with sales, this can either be the "most fun part of their job" or the most miserable as they may or may not have any comfort or confidence when engaging with the lead generation or qualification process.

When examining the skill sets of the Prospector, on the whole they tend to be more social than the Closer or Technical Expert. Their external responsibilities might include hosting client parties, generating internal newsletters or, if a senior level person, wining and dining community influencers and executives. If they are "the seasoned senior level business development person," they have been hired specifically to support executive level networking in an effort to build the type of community relationships that are fruitful for prospecting or strategic partnering.

So these are the players and their skill sets. Now that we've defined the team, let's examine what they really are doing on a day-to-day basis.

Why? Because when you participate on a team, and you do things "the way they've always been done," you may not readily identify the opportunity to improve. So for a moment give yourself the freedom to really consider the roles (defined or not) that each member plays on the sales and marketing team.

Who is on your team? Whether you are part of a one or two person team, or part of an extended team, think about each member and the skills they tend to most naturally bring to the table. Consider each person individually. Who brings in the leads? Answers technical questions? And who is effective at negotiations or closing?

Ask yourself, what role do I play in supporting the team? What's the expectation associated with my role? *What talents do I naturally feel comfortable using?* If you are a Lone Ranger, what core skills do you have? What tends to come easily to you, and what do you tend to really struggle with?

Only by really "considering the obvious" can we then move forward to examine the effectiveness of the process (you consciously or unconsciously) participate in.

Chapter Three

Four Key Phases...
And the Three Key Roles Associated with Sales.

*(Drum roll please)...*Yes, industry has a specific sales process that supports business development activities. The four components of this industries sales process were identified after studying the activities of the team and what they were doing at any given time. Although it comes so naturally to those who participate in it that it may be hard to describe, it really is straight forward and simple.

At any moment, if you look around your company at the sales team they are doing typically one of four things. They are engaged with outbound contacts, gathering information to identify new leads or business opportunities (generating leads).
They are asking questions of these potential sources of work to determine if the lead is legitimate (lead qualification).
They are frantically preparing proposals and drilling for the sales presentation (the actual sales pitch).
And they're either scratching their heads, comparing notes as to why they did not close a deal, or toasting their beers in unison if they did- (post-sales).

Again, the four things all sales teams do at all times whether they realize it or not: Lead generation, lead qualification, "the sales pitch" and post-sales activity.

This chapter is a general overview of the entire process. I will discuss each of the four phases in general terms, then in the following chapters will review in greater detail specific roles and responsibilities necessary to execute each phase as we examine more closely what is required for implementation.

Phase One: Lead Generation-
This is a fancy name for the time you dedicate and the efforts you make to find prospects and leads when they don't easily identify themselves. In simplest terms, it's what you do to try to find new business opportunities.

This phase is where you can identify qualified prospects and new opportunity leads, making them aware of the products and services that your company offers. The definition of "lead generation" is the effort you make as a team to identify prospects that actually have plans and are motivated to <u>do something</u> in terms of renovation, building or relocating (or engaging with architectural or engineering services).

Developing a MAP™ to guide our efforts.
What activities should you prioritize to find the prospects? How can you strategically organize your team prior to heading out the door, or before getting on the phone? Before you get started, you need to develop a Marketing Action Plan™ (or MAP™).

It may sound complicated, but it's really a very simple document. Your MAP™ will feature two sections: the first section is titled, "What We Know," and the second is titled, "What We Don't Know."

Essentially, in this document you will identify old fishing holes and new fishing holes, helping you to choose where to focus your efforts as a team. I'll go more into the details of how to develop the focus of your MAP™ later, but for now understand that before you begin, you should develop a strategic plan to help every member of the team focus their time and energy over a 12-month period.

Priorities of Phase One- Lead Generation

In this phase, you will try to identify who the decision makers are, what they plan to do and understand generally their timeline and motivation to take this action. From an outbound marketing standpoint, lead generation can take the form of PR events designed to expose the firm to new prospects, aggressive work site signage, direct mail or newsletters or other forms of outbound advertising investments designed to drive brand awareness. From a purely sales standpoint, lead generation is defined as the effort to actually talk to new or existing contacts in the marketplace, ask for referrals, and generate new prospects or project leads.

This is a minor difference in perspective, but often times it can become a sensitive issue as the as the "marketer" suddenly finds it their responsibility to personally assist in sales or lead generation. Often, in smaller companies, the call is issued for "all hands on deck" to help with sales; this is where there can be much frustration if the marketer/admin support/"bird dog" is **unprepared** or not properly trained in methods to effectively engage with the outbound prospecting efforts.

Although most marketers have been trained to believe that prospects would line up to do business with the industry if properly "marketed" to, the truth is that a majority of companies do not have the budgets necessary to generate effective brand awareness or positioning. This reality creates a vacuum that must be filled by ongoing and continual outbound prospecting and personal communication efforts in order to keep the prospect pipeline predictably full.

Creating the Predictable Prospect Pipeline

This notion of "keeping the prospect pipeline predictably full" is where most small- to mid-sized firms *really* struggle. To be profitable, companies must run lean on internal resources. In good times, when companies have a lot of work in the pipeline, it means everyone is very busy and is putting together proposals and running jobs, the team is focused on operational fire-fighting.

Legitimately, very few people, if anyone, in the company really has the time to invest in "prospecting." This is fine until one day, something that was a "done deal" doesn't come through and suddenly, people are scrambling for new business. As one of my clients said sarcastically, "One day we are working like mad just to keep the big jobs running, and the next, we are considering building chicken coops just to keep the doors open."

This is no way to function, yet it is a norm for companies struggling with no formal approach to their sales or business development process. One challenge Principals face is requiring the discipline and focus their team needs to continually feed the prospect pipeline, in good times and bad.

This posture of continual prospect identification requires exceptional discipline and focus, which isn't easy, but can be done. I was asked by an interviewer one time what the toughest part of business development is. My answer was that when a company is running lean (read: profitable) and has reached a degree of success, it is hard to find the time required to generate even three **qualified** new prospects or leads a week.

Imagine if every member of your team did this? Wouldn't it be wonderful?

Then why is it so terribly difficult?

It's difficult for two reasons. The first is the issue of defining truly **new** prospects. New people and contacts are hard to come by when you are in a comfort zone and have achieved a level of success, surrounded by familiar associates. So how do you push yourself out of the comfort zone?

Only through team accountability and planning- <u>where everyone knows where they are going and why they are doing what they are doing</u>- will anyone ever leave a zone of comfort for the unfamiliar. The second reason that finding three qualified new prospects a week is difficult is the issue of "qualification."

How do you know when you've got a *truly* qualified prospect?

Let's stop focusing for a moment on new prospects we want to identify, and simply review the prospects you are currently working with to convert to new customers. How many leads in your current prospect list are <u>truly</u> qualified? By "qualified," I mean this: Ready to do something, financing in place, and motivated to make a decision.

See what I mean? These are rare leads. You've got to go through a lot of unqualified people, asking focused questions, to really identify the qualified leads. This takes effort, a lot of effort.

With these issues on the table, the four-phase program I am describing to you addresses specifically the dilemmas that most firms struggle with in attempting to leverage *precious* internal resources during times of strategic growth. In an ideal world, companies have effective ad campaigns and marketers that can drive qualified prospects and leads to the door. I readily acknowledge that there are many national companies that have reached this goal through sophisticated marketing means.

For the rest of the companies, you need a real-world solution. You need a Plan B. In Phase One: Lead Generation, the members of your team will develop and follow a short-term action plan, driven by a more comprehensive strategic Marketing Action Plan(MAP™); that will help your company focus on the efforts it takes to generate qualified leads, using the very limited internal resources available (the typical three members of the sales team I've already described).

Phase Two: Lead Qualification-

A step often skipped by firms eager to "move on to the next job or get to the proposal," this is a critical phase in the process. In Phase Two, you intentionally try to slow down the race to the proposal to question and review the information and understandings that you associate with each prospect.

You should do this to determine <u>a priority of internal time investment before you move forward to invest further resources.</u> In Phase One, you identified companies and decision makers that will be "doing something." In Phase Two, you must ask more detailed and specific questions to effectively assess the prospect's needs and knowledge, and to position your version of "the sales pitch" to the decision maker.

In the book, *You Can't Learn To Ride A Bike At A Seminar*, David Sandler asserts that if you don't approach a prospect with a clearly defined sales process, they will revert to their own process. I completely agree with him, and it's in the Lead Qualification phase that you have to lay out the ground rules of engagement with the prospect so that you can clearly manage their expectations. If you don't aggressively manage the prospect from the first point of contact, it is almost guaranteed that they will default to their own primary interest– that being the issue of price.

In Phase Two: Lead Qualification, you ask several questions over a span of time to review <u>the likelihood of the prospect to buy or engage with your services in a reasonable and timely manner</u>. Once you know which prospects will doing something, you need to ask further questions to <u>prioritize</u> your efforts with them. At every point of contact in Phase Two, you take control of the process, not them. You have expectations of each planned meeting interaction, and you can decide at the conclusion of each interaction if the prospect truly merits more of the front end investment leading to a proposal.

YOU assert control of the process, not them.

How many times do you attend meetings with prospects where you are rushing to do architectural drawings or site assessments, when it isn't clear exactly what the budget or timeline is, or when a decision will be made on a sales proposal?

Phase Two is intentionally designed to <u>slow things down</u> so that critical understandings, disclosures and *trust* can be established between the contractor and decision maker, so that by the time the prospect actually enters the "sales pitch" in Phase Three, closing the deal is simple. The communications ground work and tough questions have already been addressed. So, here are the eight critical questions your team will focus on learning the answer to for each prospect in Phase Two:

1.   What is the timeline for the project?

2. What is the budget? What are the assumptions about price? How do they define "value"? Is the financing in place?

3. Who is the Decision Maker?

4. What specific criteria will they use to select a contractor partner in review of the proposal?

5. Who is the competition? What is their history with the prospect?

6. Have we addressed the proprietary nature of the solution we will provide?

7. What is the timeline for a decision to be made once the proposal is submitted?

8. What are our next steps to move the client through the pipeline, or take them out? What is the agenda for the next client meeting?

In a proper sales pitch, the third phase initiates when a request for proposal submission date has been set. While you consider the purpose of Phase Two, I challenge you further to think about this other simple rule....

There are only two types of buyers of your services- inexperienced buyers and experienced buyers.

The "inexperienced" prospect, or inexperienced construction (architectural or engineering) services buyer, has not bought these services before, so they have no frame of reference for the types of issues that must be addressed for the process to move forward smoothly. In basic terms, they have no idea what can hurt them and are typically uneducated (or unaware) of the complexity of the issues that must be addressed. They may have **no idea** about the level of detail and effort required for a comprehensive estimate, and they may be **very naive** to the issues that determine project pricing.

These are the prospects that sometimes view the activity of dealing with contractors as a "price" or negotiation game. They sometimes will perceive all contractors as "the same" and may mistake the purpose of requesting a proposal as "an opportunity to bid" in order to position one firm against another in terms of price.

Often the challenge in dealing with someone unfamiliar with building processes is slowing them down enough to give you the opportunity to credibly address the "myths" that they may believe. Here are the top five myths you have to address and overcome when managing an inexperienced prospect:

Top Five Myths in Dealing with an Inexperienced Prospect

1.   All contractors are the same.
2.   Everything comes down to price.
3.   Everything is negotiable.
4.   I can take all the time I need to do this.
5.   I have needs that are completely unique.

(These myths ought to be printed on tee-shirts and distributed at industry tradeshows).

The second type of prospect is the "experienced" prospect. This prospect has bought services similar to yours before and is coming to you with a mental frame of reference regarding that experience. Although they are an experienced prospect, you need to keep in mind that "something has happened"- otherwise they probably wouldn't be talking to you.

Outside of a geographic move, this prospect was obviously unsatisfied or unhappy with their previous experience, otherwise they would probably be working with the same vendor they originally worked with. This presents its own set of unique communication challenges. The challenge is three-fold.

Top Three Issues In Dealing with an Experienced Prospect

Facetime = Trust: They have had some type of experience and you need them to trust you enough to truthfully tell you the details of what happened. This requires "face time" with the prospect in order to develop a relationship.

Probe for Pain: You need them to tell you about their "pain"– what they are trying to overcome or change in the process of working with someone new or someone else.

Manage Their Expectations: You need to have them disclose their perceptions of how the process should occur, so that you can effectively manage or alter their expectations about price, proprietary disclosure and competition.

For these two types of prospects, there are specific communication tactics you should use to address the issues- we will go into this in greater detail shortly. What's important to remember is that your goal throughout the qualification process is to establish rapport and properly assess where the prospect is on the education or assumptions curve. Additionally, you must ask the eight key questions to confirm that they have the authority and finances (or budget) in place to make a decision.

Once qualified, you need to continue to meet with the client to invest time in the educational process, expectation management and bonding process in order to establish the trust that this kind of business transaction requires. No one writes a million dollar check to a company contact they've just met; it simply doesn't happen.

Throughout Phase Two, the goal is to engage with the prospect in structured meetings designed to meet the prospect's educational or disclosure needs, providing you the critical "face time" in which to establish credibility and trust.

In the "sales pitch," the prospect asks for a proposal submission (or a Request for Proposal) and gives you a deadline for your proposal.

Phase Three: The Sales Pitch

Throughout this text, the definition I'm presenting for the sales pitch starts and stops with specific parameters. The true "sales pitch" only begins when we have a fully qualified lead and a request for proposal deadline date has been set.

A lead does not transfer to Phase Three– "the sales pitch"– until you've had preliminary communications (or meetings) to qualify them (answer the eight questions in Phase Two) and they've indicated that you will be asked to submit a proposal for services. If you've qualified them, and there is no date for a proposal to be generated- they are still outside the official "sales pitch."

One of the first things I do with a new client when I conclude training is to review their current "hot lead" list. What I find more often than not is that many leads that are suspected to be "in the sales pipeline" are in fact, not.

Many of the leads considered "hot" or "likely to happen" aren't even fully qualified. Take a look again at the eight critical questions I list in Phase Two.

How many of the leads in your current pipeline would you say have answered in detail all eight questions? Although these questions are so obvious, many companies manage to skip critical questions in a rush to get a proposal on the table.

Often, when reviewing my client's "hot leads" list, I discover that the prospect has said they'll be building or engaging with the process "sometime"- but the critical questions relating to a timeline, budget and decision-making process relating to the review of a submitted proposal haven't been addressed.

The payoff to adhering to Phases One & Two of this system is that, by the time the prospect actually reaches Phase Three, you've laid the foundation of critical communications and understandings necessary to position your firm to "close the deal." I'll be going into further details about specific tactical approaches that you can take to manage the communications process, but consider for now the importance of actually adhering to a definitive process and the advantages that it will deliver.

Phase Four: Post-Sales Activity

At this point in the process, you pause as a team to review your internal performance in adhering to your own sales process. This is the phase where you debrief, survey new clients and lost prospects, and look to identify areas for continual team improvement.

My experience with small- to mid-sized companies (even large firms) is that most are moving so quickly, they rarely take the time to debrief and learn from their selling experiences. Unfortunately, they repeat the same errors time and time again, and valuable learning is lost.

If you doubt the value of post-sales efforts, consider the following questions:

- How do you as a company, or as a team, learn from your mistakes?
- What tools do you currently use to record the perceptions that a prospect has about the quality of your performance, the value of your proposal?
- How do you ask the delicate questions that probe the "reasoning" for the decision that they made?
- What tools do you use, or processes to maintain positive impressions once you've lost a deal?
- How do you currently secure the investment you've made in a new relationship, regardless of whether they convert to a client on this round of new business?

If you don't have solid answers to these questions, it's time to consider how you can slow down long enough to stop replicating errors that cost you dearly.

In summary, the problem most companies face when executing the phases I've identified is that the process that is "natural to the rainmaker" places the bulk of the responsibility for lead generation, qualification **and** close activity on the most valuable asset to the organization- the Closer. Why is the person with the most valuable closing and technical skills out working to generate leads? **This is exactly the reverse of the way it should be.**

Instead of the lead generation efforts originating from the most valuable person in the organization, the leads should come from someone who can afford to invest quality time to "leverage the human brand."

The challenge then becomes how to best utilize the less expensive marketing support to create a more highly functional system. How do you provide the sales person, "bird dog" or intern with the communication skills or processes appropriate to become truly effective in the area of lead generation?

Although my experience with Closers and Rainmakers indicates that they will typically never fully let go of the lead generation activities (and they really shouldn't, since they are so effective at it), they <u>will</u> relinquish control <u>to the degree of confidence</u> they have in other options. They require a finely honed and dependable system, one that is not dependent on any one given person.

The Exit Strategy Issue

You see, as long as most of the lead generation efforts originate from the desk of the Rainmaker, the exit strategy for the company is seriously compromised. There must be in place a self-sustaining system that diverts the pressure of lead generation from the Rainmaker to other organizational talent. **It needs to be a system that's completely sustainable and not dependent on the skills or relationships of any one individual.** This is the problem companies face when they desire growth and determine that the best way in which to accomplish growth is through the hiring of a "Senior Level" Business Development person.

Although a reasonable short-term solution, the problem arises again in the simple fact that any Senior Level person that you hire can leave at any time. Worse, if they do leave, they take their contacts with them. Simply hiring the "Senior Level Talent" does not ensure you that will create an independent sales system that manages the intellectual property associated with the company. Companies need a more comprehensive and long-term solution to this issue, which is the core priority of the program which I'm describing.

Let's look at a diagram describing the ideal self-sustaining system on the following page. This the way it should look.

So how do you transition your team from here to there? How do you make the organizational and cultural shift necessary to make the transition– to actually get everyone working throughout the four phases to perform in a seamless rhythm? To answer this question, you need to re-assess each member participating on the sales team and clarify their roles and responsibilities. For my original client, we approached this issue by applying an organizational template I've developed called **CODE.**

CODE is an acronym for the following key questions that each company must answer in executing the sales process. CODE stands for:

> **Communication: How do we communicate *externally* with prospects? How do we communicate *internally* to coordinate our efforts as a team?**
> **Organization: How do we organize our resources?**
> **Documentation: How do we document our progress?**
> **Evaluation: How do we evaluate our performance?**

In applying CODE to the four phases, I focused on the development of management tools and templates to train the team to execute consistently each phase of the CODE sales process.

I sensed that if a company could outline in a step-by-step process the answers for each of the questions contained in CODE, then they could more consistently execute and monitor each step of the sales process.

50

Overview of CODE®

The Prospect Pool
- Defined by the MAP
- Short Term Plans determine monthly priorities

Phase 1: Lead Generation

Yellow Leads = 18–24 months

- Basic Yellow
- Yellow
- Blue
- Red

Prospector

Phase 2: Lead Qualification
- Educate or Find Pain
- Answer 8 Key Questions
- Blues Leads = 12–18 months

- Blues
- Reds

Technical Expert

RFP Date Indicated

Phase 3: Sales Process
- Red Leads Convert
- Red Leads = 0 –12 months

Team & Closer

Phase 4: Post Sales Activity
- Survey / De-brief
- New customer = Project Start-Up

A good analogy for CODE is comparing it to a DNA sequence that determines the characteristics inherent to a business. If a company has a poorly defined CODE, its DNA will dictate the performance accordingly- **say to that of a monkey.**

If a company has a well-defined CODE, the DNA sequence becomes stronger and the company can perform at a higher level, **more like a gorilla.** The clearer the CODE, the more a company sales team can replicate and focus on what's working for their team.

So what does your team want to be? A monkey or a gorilla? I vote for the gorilla.

The true beauty of CODE became clear when, after my first official training, a sales team reported a breakthrough understanding of what was expected of them in their role. They knew how to report to management and monitor their progress. They could identify and troubleshoot key communication issues with clients. And perhaps most importantly, members of the team became more **satisfied** with their role and "job" in general, as it was obvious that management **was committed** to helping them succeed.

The core philosophy behind CODE is that nobody plans to come to work and fail. No one wakes up one morning saying, "Today is the day I want to under-perform."

However, people do show up and under perform in sales and business development all the time. Why is this? Usually it's not that they plan on not meeting management's expectations. It's that they haven't been trained properly, or they were improperly hired in the first place- as there were no specific and clear performance expectations expressed in the interview phase.

As you consider the elements of CODE, ask yourself, how would your company answer the questions posed in CODE currently? In lead generation efforts, how do you communicate with prospects? In qualifying prospects, how do you organize your team? In the sales process, how do you evaluate your performance?

Ponder these issues as we move to explore more closely what is required in executing Phase One, Lead Generation.

Chapter Four

Welcome to Phase 1: Lead Generation

It's time for the magic of show and tell

In considering how to get started, you should consider each question posed by CODE, starting with Communication-How do you externally communicate while generating leads or going out to find new business?

With limited time and money, what's the most cost effective way to generate leads? *Where do you go to find prospects that won't identify themselves?* When they won't necessarily come to you, <u>you need to go to them</u>.

In one of my earliest experiences with my initial client, I discovered something that flat out *blew* my mind. Please allow me a moment to reminisce with you.

It's 98 degrees and another painfully humid July day in the Midwest. My client had asked me to physically visit the job site of a building that they were working on that was being constructed in the method of tilt-up concrete. Now I had seen buildings before, but my client wanted me to take a close look at this one because it was an example of an "instant" building. One moment, it was not there...and the next, through the magic of panel erection, the structure appeared almost instantly.

They wanted me to experience first-hand the "wow factor" of an instant building, and they also wanted me to observe the reaction of strategic partners (architects and developers) that they'd invited to come view the spectacle.

Ok,. I could do this even if the humidity meant a bad hair day.

When I arrived, I walked to the site where, yes, in a matter of moments a building began to appear. Wow!

*While we were casually standing there, a man **actually** walked up to the worksite, business card in hand and asked, "Would you have someone call me? We are looking at building options, and I have been impressed with the management of this site."*

I casually glanced around and muttered, "Alright, who sent this guy....Who's messing with the consultant... This is a joke, right?"

***The joke was on me**. You see, this gentleman had been watching the site **for months** from a building across the way. He'd seen it **every day** as he came and went from his office window. As the construction began, he was terribly curious who his new neighbors would be. Being a business owner, maybe they could be customers? Maybe they could be strategic partners? Who really knew?*

All he knew for sure was that for months, there was a constant ruckus that piqued the curiosity of everyone in the business park. Whether I realized it or not, the entire geographic surrounding area was filled with other business people, decision makers and influencers, intrigued by the sudden activity going on in a formerly vacant lot.

Introducing "The Cereal Box Effect"

Since my original encounter with this phenomenon, I've come to lovingly refer to this as "the cereal box effect". You know how it is when someone places a cereal box in the middle of a table? You try to avoid reading the silly box, but before long...out of boredom, curiosity or whatever....you just start reading the box.

You don't mean to. You may not even want to. But with the bright colors, the pictures and the zippy graphics– you are sucked in. Unless there's a newspaper at the table, I can tell you more about the Batman promotion on Cheerios than I would ever care to admit.

This is the same thing I've witnessed with construction sites. People in the surrounding business, industrial and office parks get curious. <u>Very curious.</u> *They want to know what's going on, who's moving in, what's happening and when.* The longer the site is under development, the more curious people are. *They can't help it.* It is natural human nature when you walk by, drive by and look at something all the time. You simply begin to wonder about it.

The man who casually stopped by to drop off his card had been studying the site for months. Daily, he'd watched to observe how clean it was, when the workmen showed up, and was really impressed when all of a sudden, due to tilt-up technology, there was an "instant" building. *WOW!*

What a way to legitimize a brand! Show the product and capitalize on the natural curiosity of business people (read: decision makers).

What I'm describing for you is an ultimate game of <u>show and tell</u>. On the site I visited with my client, I was mortified when I reviewed the condition of the signage. Here we had a captive audience within a 3 to5 mile radius – with 40-foot trailers just blankly sitting there! Sure, they had a sun-bleached logo from the 1970s....but that was it.

Here at our disposal we had huge, mobile billboards with little to nothing interesting to say to our captive audience!! It was totally ridiculous. If my client were to glance at the freeway within a few hundred feet of the site, a simple billboard would have cost *thousands of dollars.*

Here, on ground that he controlled, we had very limited and poorly done site signage. *Ouch.*

Even though it is as obvious as an 40-foot billboard, how many times do you drive by sites with little to no clear signs? It's baffling. I realize that most areas have regulations that direct the use of signs, but still- every single company out there ought to ask, *how effective are the signs at our sites? On our trucks?* How *consistent and bold* is our brand and message at every point of prospect or customer interface? This goes for you, too, Architects and Engineers. How compelling is *your site* signage and trucks? How abstract or generally difficult to read is your "brand" if you pass by it over one mile an hour?

We found that by creating an entertaining and rapidly changing series of communication "billboards," we could carry on a virtual conversation with surrounding business community.

Stop and think about the times you've been sitting at an airport or walking down the street and someone in the crowd starts talking in a loud voice about politics, religion... or whatever else is on their mind. Whether you like it or not, you are stuck listening. You are captive. On the hot Missouri day, I realized we had an audience, and they were listening. We just needed to talk louder and more clearly.

And for goodness sake, we needed to say something *interesting!*

I continued to ponder the situation. If this man had identified himself out of the clear blue, *how many others were out there?* How many other decision makers in the immediate geographic area were considering renovation or building?

I sat and thought about our options to reach them. Yes, we could do direct mail...but it's passive, as it relies on them to do work to further the relationship- and they don't know us from Adam. My client had essentially already proved that direct mail probably wasn't going to work.

Over the course of the night I kept asking myself, how could we <u>effectively</u> reach them? *Really reach them??*

The first step was to aggressively re-do all the site signage and apply stickers to all of the tailgates of our trucks, using a funny and personal message. None of this "quality is job one" stodgy crap. Instead, I had my brilliant friend and copywriter come up with a number of witty "billboards" that we'd rotate every other week to keep the audience interested. Some of the billboards included:

"Mom Always Said Go Do Something Constructive" (with strong logo and website)

"We Build Things, Relationships For Starters"

"Hard hats, Not Hard Heads"

"Those Neighbor Boys Are At It Again"

"It's Hard Keeping Up With The Neighbors"

"Sure we're competitive. We're brothers."

As you can tell, these weren't earth-shattering sentiments...*but they were darn good.* They captured an unusual and gutsy feel that's not typical for a construction company. They take a funny and not-so-serious slant, one that makes it worth reading to folks passing by.

I went to the next client meeting with a plan in hand. Now this was gutsy...

"Okay Gentlemen...After yesterday's fabulous revelation, I've identified an aggressive strategy. Let's actually go to the prospects! Yes, let's do something rare: let's introduce *ourselves as neighbors!* Let's drop off the "cup of sugar" (some candy or desk ornament) and stop by to talk to our business park neighbors about the new company moving in down the block, and our services. *Let's invite our new friends to meet their new neighbor and visit further with them about their plans for the future of their company."*

(Wow... I was so excited and could not wait to hear their reaction.)

My three members of the client team just kind of sat there for a moment and studied me. They had to take a moment to digest this. From the looks on their faces I could read the reaction...*Come on now. Surely I wasn't being literal.*

I wasn't suggesting walking into offices out of the blue? Was I? No, she couldn't possibly mean it.

They kept looking at me.. .I locked their gaze.

Was she completely bonkers?

Being the sensitive leader and soft-spoken person that my client is, he gently asked..."Elizabeth, who will actually do this? Who has the time?" I knew from his eyes the answer. He **certainly** didn't have the time. He was the Rainmaker and Closer.

His Construction Division President (Technical Expert) certainly didn't have the time either. That left the marketing administrator with the short straw, who in less than a split second understood exactly where this was headed.

"You cannot be serious," was the look on his face. (This was going to be fun....and yes, to his astonishment, I was serious.)

Moving Out of the Comfort Zone

Now let's bounce back to reality for a moment. The idea of going out– leaving your comfortable office– to prospect sounds *daunting*, even sometimes for the most seasoned sales person. Imagine how it sounded to an intern- who REALLY didn't sign up for this crap. He was doing website updates, proposal assembly...*not cold calls!* Who was I to suggest this change in course?

Well, fortunately I'm just the crazy consultant, not a full time employee- so I could suggest about anything without facing daily scrutiny. Here we were at a critical junction. The idea sounded intriguing- but the reality...*Not so tasty*.

What would happen if we actually did it? Here's what happened...

Once the poor lad got over the initial shock of the request, he flat out told me he wasn't dining on the dog food alone. Nope, I was to go with him on his first prospecting activities. We would walk as a pair, going door to door in business parks, manufacturing areas and industrial parks in areas where we had current jobs or past jobs.

So, what happened? Several things.

Titles Do Make a Difference In Getting Past Gatekeepers

During the course of events, we tried on several different titles for him to introduce himself. (Since most companies have a "gatekeeper" or secretary/administrative person at the front desk, getting this person comfortable with our presence was our first hurdle.) Titles we considered for ourselves when we walked in included:

Business Development Director
Sales Manager, or
Marketing Manager

These sounded official enough and convincing enough to be credible. In testing the reactions that "Gatekeepers" had to these titles, we discovered that they really weren't working well; each time, we were viewed as "sales people" or possibly even solicitors.

Sometimes they would listen, and some-times we would be shut down before we got started. Just as we'd explain the purpose of the visit, they'd politely (or not so politely) suggest we leave a card and move along.

So after our sixth attempt or so, I suggested we try something else. I thought, if they think "sales" with these titles, let's give them something they can't easily peg. Let's try something weird, almost a not-for-profit title...one that's elusive, but accurate.

Let's try the crazy title "Community Relations Director" for the Prospector. Let's walk in, introduce ourselves as the Community Relations Director for my client's construction firm, and ask if we can speak with someone about their lease or facility. We'll focus on walking the areas surrounding our current worksites, and walk in to introduce ourselves to our new neighbors with building "footprints" that make sense. We'll invite them to an open house for our new building grand opening, ask them to come meet other neighbors and network with others businesses from the surrounding area. After this, we'll also ask them a few simple questions about their lease (when it's up, if they are considering renovations or know of companies in the vicinities that are).

Sounds really "Martha Stewart," doesn't it? Neighbors talking to neighbors, casual chatting and invitations to open houses. Really odd for construction companies.

What we discovered is that with the Community Relations Director title, the Gatekeeper really had no idea what our intentions were. It wasn't readily obvious. Sure, we could be sales. But the title didn't sound "sales-y."

Nope, they would have to visit with us a little. And the longer they did, typically the more we learned about them. Within ten minutes, we usually could discover when their lease was up, and if they intended to build or renovate.

Oftentimes we discovered that the Gatekeeper was in direct earshot of the Decision Maker.

If we made a favorable impression on the Gatekeeper, then the Decision Maker would pop his or her head out of the opposing office to meet us personally, as they were curious and inclined to learn more about the details of the company moving in up the street. It seems appropriate to mention at this time that not all of my clients choose to apply this title to the Prospector role, but that trial and error does support that it is effective. Ultimately it's up to the firm to determine if the title is a cultural good fit, but the issue of how the title is perceived by the gatekeeper is an important aspect to consider.

Prospecting Defined

The primary goal of Phase One is purely making favorable "first contact" with potential prospects. **We wanted them to connect a face and name to the construction company building up the street (the human brand).** We wanted to make a very kind and favorable impression- and we wanted to walk out with the business card of someone we could talk to about the building, lease or renovation needs of the company. For our efforts, we held to three golden rules that defined a successful prospecting visit.

The Three Golden Rules of Prospecting:
1. Make a favorable impression.
2. Meet the gatekeeper and get the business card of the decision maker.
3. Ask key questions and document the information about their future plans for the office or lease.

If we accomplished these three things, we considered the prospecting effort a success. From the scope of the questions, you can see we did not obtain every detail necessary to determine the viability of the contact. No, we simply gained enough information so that further phone-based qualification efforts could be made.

Should the contact be talkative, we would ask further questions. In most instances though, we just sought to be friendly and obtain as much information as we felt comfortable asking.

Most importantly, during the interaction we worked to introduce the name of the construction company, mention the name of their new neighbor- and typically invite them to an open house to celebrate the move-in, and meet more neighbors. We did this to gauge their interest in our company, and to provide further face time appropriate to additional questions. Results of our prospecting efforts were transferred into a simple color coded system designed to help us manage leads and further develop the prospect pipeline.

Now as you think about this, don't get the impression I'm suggesting your business development team should wander aimlessly around business parks or industrial centers.

That is not what I'm suggesting at all.

What I am suggesting is that you do your online research in advance to identify prospects or companies that are viable candidates within a 3-5 mile radius of your firm's worksites, and that you simply take the time to get off the derriere to go meet them and say hello.

In the old days, an industrial salesmen I've known used to call this activity "smoke-stacking." Getting out of your office and actually looking for companies with "smoke-stacks." Meaning: actively reviewing geographic areas appropriate to identify companies with the "smokestack" appropriate to fit the profile of a buying prospect. It's an old technique, that with the use of today's technology (advance online research)- it is still very effective.

People getting out meeting other people and doing business with people they like. (Now there's an innovative idea.)

Color Categorizing the Prospects
Our goal once we attained the basic prospect, lead or opportunity information was to categorically label and assign the leads into the following color-based categories: Yellow, Blue and Red.

Categories for each lead generated in Phase One

> **Yellow Basic:** When you categorize a lead as Yellow Basic, you have obtained basic information to know the company will be "doing something within the next 18-24 months," but you need more detailed answers before you could say with confidence that they were a "fully qualified" Yellow lead. Consider a Yellow basic to be similar to "hear say."

For example, if you walk in and learn that a firm is going to renovate, but you do not get the name of the decision maker or when it will happen- you would assign the lead into the Yellow Basic category, which means that the Prospector needs to contact the business for further follow-up. You have identified a need to acquire key informational details necessary to move the lead to the Yellow category. Once the questions have been answered, the Yellow Basic becomes a true "Yellow."

> **Yellow:** This label is applied to any company that has said *definitively* that they are moving forward in the next 18 to 24 months with new building construction, renovation or change of location (lease expiration).

For prospect or lead to be categorized as a Yellow, you've gathered the following basic information:
- Business Name
- Address
- Gatekeeper Name
- Type of Business/ Type of Industry
- Decision Maker Name
- Years in Business
- Expansion Plans
- Satisfaction With Location/ Facilities
- Lease Length/ Anticipated Moving Date/ Sq. Foot Required

- Other Anticipated Change(s) in Near Future
- Referral Name of Other Companies with Similar Needs

Again, the definition of a Yellow lead is that they are doing something. We really don't know all the details and need a real meeting with them to learn more. A lot more. When the Yellow will accept a meeting with us and is confirmed to "be doing something"– then the Yellow lead becomes a Blue lead.

Yellow to Blue Transfer: Note that until it is confirmed by the Prospector that there is a confirmed interest in this initial qualification and fact finding meeting, the lead remains a Yellow. Once you confirm that there is interest in a meeting, and an agenda and time for the meeting has been set- the lead transfers from a Yellow to a Blue.

> **Blue:** A Blue lead is any lead or prospect that has confirmed that they will be renovating, building or expanding their facilities in the next 18 to 24 months, *and there is a confirmed meeting date set.*

A Blue lead can be moving faster than the 18 to 24 month time span, but the key is that they are confirmed to be "doing something" and will accept a first meeting designed to further qualify them, learn their motivations, intentions, level of experience and assumptions about pricing, budgets and proprietary solutions. While leads are considered Blue, there are eight key qualification questions that are explored in depth. These questions are absolutely critical and constitute the bulk of the efforts we make in Phase Two, Lead Qualification. They are:

1. What is the timeline for the project?

2. What is the budget? What are the assumptions about price? How do they define "value"? Is the financing in place?

3. Who is the Decision Maker?

4. What specific criteria will they use to select a contractor partner in review of the proposal?

5. Who is the competition? What is their history with the prospect?

6. Have we addressed the proprietary nature of the solution we will provide?

7. What is the timeline for a decision to be made once the proposal is submitted?

8. What are our next steps to move the client through the pipeline, or take them out? What is the agenda for the next client meeting?

Blue to Red Transfer: Once a prospect has been fully qualified and a request for proposal (RFP) due date has been set, then the Blue lead transfers to a Red. Based on these criteria, a Blue prospect may remain a Blue for many "joint qualification meetings," or only a few.

The critical factors determining a Blue to Red transfer is that the eight qualification questions have been answered and an RFP date has been indicated.

Red: A Red lead is any lead that is confirmed to be building, renovating or moving in the next 0-12 months, will accept a meeting, and has indicated a date for an RFP.

As you can tell, the Red lead is "red hot." They often have multiple parties competing for the job, are at the final stages of decision making, and are considered low-hanging fruit. Although Reds are desirable to fill the prospect pipeline, the Reds are notoriously competitive and difficult to manage in terms of gaining a competitive edge. Why? Because Reds naturally tend to be moving very fast, which means that you have little time to establish the relationship and differentiate your company from the competition. They are desirable but typically tough to manage unless you have an inside track.

Proactivity = Predictability
The purpose of Phase 1 is to provide your company with ample Yellow and Blue leads, so that a company has both the time and options when it comes to assessing the position that they want to take with Red leads. The advantage of this proactive posture is that it provides a good pipeline of well qualified leads- so that your team can be selective about the types of business you want to service, or how competitive you want to be for the Reds that are "out there."

The goal of any prospecting activity is to make contact with the Decision Maker, ask a few questions, leave a favorable impression, and then continue to stay in contact to gather further information or enhance the "relationship" opportunity. Depending on where the lead is in their awareness and urgency, these factors determine further how the lead is handled.

For example, should the Prospector identify a Red lead that requires immediate attention, the Principal or "Closer" would be called to immediately follow up with the contact. If on the other hand, the Prospector identifies a Blue lead – one that has indicated a desire for further education on construction options (for example)- then the Prospector would set the meeting and transfer or work directly with the Technical Expert who will address the prospect's desired agenda.

Through continual review of the color coded pipeline, the Prospector uses his judgment (with support of his seasoned team) to determine where the prospect is in the decision-making process. The goal of the Prospector in Phase One is to generate qualified leads and transfer them to the Technical Expert when the Yellow expresses a desire for further meetings, becoming a Blue.

Timely Information Is the Asset
Are you starting to get the picture? I discovered that, with good planning, we could go out and canvass a geographic area around our active worksites, gathering critical business intelligence about companies that might become real "prospects"– prospects that would or could be building or "doing something" in the next 18 to 24 months.

Attaining this type of information did not take the President of the company walking in. It simply took someone with the time and interest to pursue it– someone dedicated to turning up leads, someone who liked going out and networking with other businesses in a meaningful fashion, trying to set up new business contacts.

Ideally, you need someone who could be described as a "Rush Chairman" type of personality- young, assertive and friendly. This often isn't the checklist that construction companies look for in a lead generator, but research and results suggest that this is exactly the type of person that you should be looking for.

One of the top producers using the CODE program (our national training program for this marketing approach) is based in North Dakota. He joined the team for my client as a former college intern; he wanted to help head up the prospecting efforts. Now, in reviewing this CRD's resume, he had much to be proud of. He was an Eagle Scout, demonstrated an early interest in entrepreneurship– and generally could support the declaration that throughout his life experience, he was not afraid of process or meeting new people. His disposition is bright, assertive and certainly not afraid to learn or take on steep challenges (becoming familiar with the technical skills and vocabulary required in a deeply technical industry).

He was an outstanding young man whose family and friends were committed to the local community. Within one year of running this proactive prospecting approach, the team he worked with had identified $12 million in negotiated and design build work opportunities, $6 million of which the team was able to close and convert to new revenue. He personally was credited with $1million of that total within the first year of employment. And keep in mind this other critical fact. This firm had a history of pure "hard bid." Making the jump to negotiated and design build work was a significant leap of faith for the firm- but management was committed and needed a process to bridge the gap. Fortunate for me they choose CODE.

On year two and now into year three, the team identified $22 million in total market opportunity, chose to put together proposals on $18 million, closed a total of $12 million - $6 million of which our boy wonder was given credit for. Amazing. Almost perhaps more importantly, the company has made this process so integral to their market approach that they now are very choosy about when and why they engage with the hard bid process. To say they don't miss it is an understatement.

Not too darn shabby for a company competing in North Dakota.

Who does the Prospecting work for your company?
Who is committed (meaning held accountable on a weekly basis) for continually identifying truly new contacts or new referrals? When I ask this question, often there is a very uncomfortable silence because, in essence, it's "everyone's job," if you ask the Principal of the organization– and no one's job, if you ask who specifically is accountable to do it weekly. This situation is not good. Someone has to be assigned and held responsible for the task associated with prospecting.

Too often, it never even occurs to companies that they should be proactively prospecting. They discuss frequently the issue of "networking," but that's the extent of it. What the concept of "networking" means in definitive terms and what management expects never gets formally spelled out.

Instead, it's an agreed upon "concept" in which everyone participates but no one really has the reporting or management tools with which to monitor it. It's both an activity of the sales team and a required skill of each team member. It's expected that the team "networks"- so much so that often it's an unspoken assumption. This is fine, but consider with me for a moment the dangers that are associated with the pure "network" approach to business development.

"What are you doing, dude?"
"What do you think? I'm networking."

First, if you are like most individuals, the thought of going outside your network of friends and colleagues is very scary...so you don't naturally do it. Instead, you stay vested in a group of relationships, hoping that they produce new market information, referrals and leads over time. The problem is that if you evaluate where most of these relationships exist, you'll find it's in things such as local Chambers of Commerce, Rotary Clubs, professional societies, or other structured localized groups that offer "networking" events.

This is a natural place for sales people to be. And if you are on the sales team, it is safe to assume that you are expected to take an active role in the business community networking events. I take no issue with this: attending designated events to represent your firm in the networking arena is a critical part of the sales team duties.

However, I do have an issue with the fact that the act of "networking" within established "business associations and groups" is often the only place where the team really focuses their time in search of new leads. This is friends talking to friends, which is, in many respects, the way business gets done. But let's be frank, it has some very serious limitations.

The challenge is that there is only so much room in any of these "networking ponds." There are only so many legitimate leads, and most of your competition tends to attend these events as well. Essentially, everyone is trying to identify and secure relationships with the same legitimate leads, in the same lead generation channel. Are you getting the picture?

Again, I don't want to suggest for a moment that attending these events and participating in these networking forums is unnecessary. It is a great idea, and it's essentially required of your team. However, for truly sustainable growth, it can't be the **only** thing that your team does.

You've got to move out of your comfort zone. Your team has to move out of their core contact zone and go somewhere that your competition isn't....I want to suggest strongly to you that you go directly to the customer or dream client.

This is so obvious. So, why isn't it natural for companies in the A/E/C industry? Many times, in talking to entrepreneurs and business owners, the confession that I encounter is that it is very easy to get lethargic. Once you obtain some big wins for the company, it's very easy to "lay off the lead generation efforts" because those big jobs are in the pipeline and on the back log. The other thing, is that it's just "too hard" to really help the "technical guys" become good prospectors. They don't know how, or worse- actually see little value in the process of training and actually embracing cultural change.

This reality is especially true for architects and engineering firms. Architects conceptually appreciate the idea of prospecting, but in the stark light of day tend to view it as a lack of billable time. It simply isn't a priority of the business model.

The same is also true for Engineers. In an interview with a marketing director for a national engineering firm, the project managers were frequently asked by management to actually "cut the chit chat" with clients to focus on more billable time. These are the same people- or Technical Experts, that are simultaneously expected to act as Prospectors cross-selling new projects to core customers.

Can you understand the inherent tension?

In good times of growth, it's easy for management to ignore or not deal with. **And this is when most leaders and teams will admit, that they are at their most vulnerable place: fat and too happy.** If any circumstances change or don't develop into anticipated revenue, the company quickly can find itself scrambling to fill the back log and accepting work that normally they'd balk at.

Even the most outgoing Rainmakers get lazy, tired and over-dependent upon key networks. They simply fail to replenish their sources of <u>new</u> contacts and <u>new</u> leads. As Rainmakers mature from young entrepreneurs to established business people, they will often say that in looking back, they should have just gone after their dream clients that they wish they had. They shouldn't have been scared or waited for the market to "come to them." Nope, they should have defined clearly the types of negotiated work that they wanted. They should have defined the most profitable types of work for the firm, and they should have used every tool in their bag of tricks to go out and get it.

Too frequently the prospects that are truly high-growth firms are so busy that the key managers no longer have time to attend to business forums, such as Chamber of Commerce events. No, these high-growth companies tend to show up for the "High Growth Awards Gala" and that's about it. They pick up awards for their accomplishments and head home. So why not go to them?

Get out of the room full of your "friendly competition" and hit the street. Meet and greet! Founders of any company will tell you that the key to "Rainmaking" is often taking the TIME to go OUTSIDE your comfort zone and continually meet NEW people.

Yes, it helps when your network contact makes the introduction for you, but come on, most companies get lazy and become dependent on others for that introduction. They are not out there defining their "dream clients," doing the research and getting the appointments to meet with decision makers. Instead they quietly wait for the phone to ring or the next project to be bid; you can't sustain this mindset and be effective at breaking through to the next phase of revenue growth. It just does not work. You have to get your team organized, focused and making outbound communications with contacts that otherwise they don't know.

Getting Started: Before you head out the door
Develop your 12-month Marketing Action Plan™, or a MAP™. Before you do anything, you really need a comprehensive plan that will dictate the day to day focus for your team. So to get started, you need to develop a Marketing Action Plan™ (or MAP™). It may sound complicated, but it's really a <u>very</u> simple document. The MAP™ features two sections: the first section is titled, "What We Know," and the second is titled "What We Don't Know." Simple enough!

Section One of the MAP™: What We Know
In the first section of the MAP™ that describes "What We Know," you need to develop lists of people or companies "that you know." The lists will include:
Core clients: People you need to call anyway to check in on, see how they are and ask for a referral;
Federal Government Agencies/ Municipalities
Architects: People you know that you may want to do more work with;
Developers/ Realtors: Again, folks you may know but not be doing much work for;
Accountants/Bankers/ Attorneys: Who owe you favors, always good for referrals;
Subcontractors/ Suppliers (who owe you favors);
Other strategic partners or friends and family to prioritize in the request for referrals or insider information.

In this section you might also list events or associations such as Economic Development Councils that you want to target for improved visibility and participation. Think of this section of the MAP™ as something that describes your "old fishing holes"- places, people and associations that make sense for you to focus on in asking for market information or referrals. **In reviewing this section, keep in mind that your team will invest approximately 70% of available resources (or 70% of our available time) to go after results by working with "people we know."** When you compile these lists it might be tempting to dump in data base lists the size of the yellow pages, but don't do it. Keep the lists short, manageable and realistic. You want a clean, easy to read section of the MAP™ that list out specific contacts that are of core priority to your firm. By organizing it this way, it's not overwhelming or cumbersome to review.

Let me provide a few examples relating to the "What We Know" section of the MAP™. Let's say it's up to you to contact the bankers on the list. You might contact your bankers and offer to do a "Biggest Investment" brown bag lunch seminar for their business account/ loan managers. This seminar would provide them an outline of indicators that a business is indeed qualified and ready to engage with the building, renovation or expansion process. In the seminar, you would provide them an overview of the indicators, options and issues that the banker should prepare their client for when they are faced with the question- should we build? In essence, you enable the banker to pre-qualify a business end user for you. In sharing information with them, they also enhance their value to their customers in that they become more able to articulate the process they should expect to engage with should they want to evaluate their options.

Once the seminar is offered, the prospector might follow up with the bankers quarterly to see if they've got referrals or questions you can address for them. As you can see, it's not rocket science – but there needs to be a purpose for contact and it needs to provide some tangible value for the strategic partner.

In considering other targets within the "what we know" category of the MAP™, let's also consider subcontractors. These are typically business contacts that have a lot of direct market knowledge, that desire to do more business with your firm. One of the first efforts I make when I visit with a new client is to go to accounting and to print out a list of account payables to subcontractors. Once we've got the list of the top fifteen or so subcontractors paid over the past 12 months, the prospector prioritizes outbound phone calls to the account contact asking for referral information or market knowledge- gently reminding them of the business commitment that's been made over the past 12 months.

One of my clients in an effort to adapt this concept to "policy" has made it a priority when accepting new subcontractor meetings- to communicate the expectation that in exchange for accepting the meeting, he anticipates some type of referral or intriguing market revelation to be provided. And strangely, you know what? He gets what he asks for.

What do you ask for when you meet with business contacts? As the Good Book states, "you have not because you ask not." Use every opportunity possible to query about new business or market knowledge. Through the simple rule of degrees of separation, people have access to incredible amounts of information. Train yourself to ask everyone you are in contact with...What do you know? What have you heard?

Section Two of the MAP™: What We Don't Know
The second section of your MAP focuses on prioritizing "new fishing holes"- people, places and dream clients or industries that you want to focus on to expand the

prospecting efforts. Included in this section may be geographic areas such as industrial, technology or manufacturing parks that are appropriate to target. You might also list "dream clients" or vertical industries like long-term care facilities, agricultural processing facilities, retail or other specific verticals appropriate to focus on. In both sections of the MAP™, your firm should try to define very specific objectives, goals, strategies, tactics and measures for each of the targets. It may sound difficult, but try to describe in very specific terms what you hope to achieve so that you will have a measure by which to determine whether or not you've accomplished your goal. If you are not specific in terms of your goals, it will be very difficult to monitor the accomplishments of your team- and this becomes a de-motivator for people if they can't see progress....So do this extra step in an effort to quantify your efforts.

A section on the MAP™ might look something like this:

Target: Commercial Development Firms
Objective- To establish a new working relationship with _____(name of contacts)_____ who are a developers we want to do business with.

Goal- Close at least one deal over a million dollars with one of these developers by Q3 of next year.

Strategy- We will try to meet with _____ every six to eight weeks, beginning Q1 this year to begin the process of "relationship building".

Tactics- We will set meeting agendas to review what our company can do, the projects we've already completed, and we will describe new methods we are using to create value for our clients in the design build process. We will develop one page case studies of last years key projects to present specific capabilities; and after three meetings we will introduce Principals of the firms in a effort to identify specific joint prospects appropriate for both firms to pursue.

Measures- Preparation, drive time, and face time may total 30-50 hours of time invested for each new developer contact. Our measure of success this year is a total of 3-4 meetings with our two targeted companies. We will have at least one meeting with organization Principals with the goal to identify 3 potential joint new business opportunities, 1 of which we want to close by Q3 next year.

Now, what you are looking at in this example is truly "marketing terminology". **If it concerns you, overwhelms or flat out baffles you...Don't worry**. I encourage you to use the language that you are familiar with to write simple goals for each target listed on your MAP™.

Such as :
We want to contact Bingo Architects, Davis Designers and Big Shot Developers over the next 3 months. Our goal is to identify 3 new jobs amongst these new contacts, converting one to new work. Steve Johnston is responsible to make this happen.

Weekly Progress Reporting Drives Accountability to the MAP™. Once the two sections of the MAP™ are defined, the goal for the team becomes identification of "who will do what." Through this assignment of duties, the individuals managing the MAP™ take ownership of their piece that they are responsible for.

Each team member then writes out a simple short-term plan for each target identified in the MAP™. These short-term plans are simply the monthly priorities (or productivity goals) that are reviewed weekly by the team to make sure that the MAP™ is properly being followed. Once you've got the MAP™ (a 12 month plan), and everyone is clear on their short term plan assignments (30 day priorities)- you are ready to start Phase One.

Accountability = Sustainable Results
The most important aspect of lead generation is to actually engage with your short term plan and to communicate weekly with your team your progress in managing the resulting Yellow, Blue and Red prospects. **Do what you plan to do, and communicate to others weekly your progress.** This sounds so simple, but prioritizing the meeting during the implementation phase is very difficult for already "very busy" people.

The thing you must remember is that CODE will perform <u>exactly</u> to the degree in which you implement it. Much like a diet, if you cheat and blow off weekly meetings- you are going to get sloppy and probably begin to undermine your efforts to date.

To help you understand the significance of managing your pipeline, let's say you've got 3 newly identified Yellows you've uncovered. These are prospects that say they are going to do something, we don't necessarily know what or when – they've just said things like..."My lease is coming up... we are re-thinking space issues, would consider an option like build to suit, but really haven't made a decision."

Well, we know that they'll have to make some type of decision based on their lease negotiations.... So there is a timeline in which you've got to keep in touch with them as they move toward decision making. Should you skip weekly communication meetings, the Prospector may miss important communication deadlines with the lead because it's been off their radar, resulting in missed job opportunities for the firm.

The timeliness of the information collected by the Prospector is absolutely critical- and requires aggressive management to be properly leveraged. How does this relate to performance goals? If for example on your MAP™ the Principal plans to contact 3 past customers weekly to ask for referrals, then weekly the Principal needs to report to his team the progress toward this goal.

Progress Reporting

From management's perspective, it is the Prospector's responsibility to make sure that the weekly progress meetings are a priority (that the meetings actually happen), and that those attending actually do report on their progress. The Prospector then updates the pipeline information to reflect changes and maintains a master "to do" list.

In practical terms, if you are a small business- this might mean that the Principal (Closer) is now accountable to the intern (Prospector) to report progress on his portion of the MAP™ and short-term plan. (Yes, you read that last sentence correctly.)

This may create an interesting dynamic, but holding one another accountable is a very important step to reaching the goals. From a culture perspective, this aspect of CODE is very unique. The organization of the team requires a degree of humble leadership, as the weekly reporting structure requires accountability to one another as a team- regardless of where you fall on the corporate totem pole.

Each team member should carry with them only three pieces of paper to each weekly progress meeting. The first is a weekly progress report, a second is a "to do" list specific to activities they will follow up on in the upcoming week, and the third is the color coded spread sheet identifying by category each yellow, blue and red lead. Very simple. It is the responsibility of the Prospector to show the status of the sales pipeline using the one-page progress report focusing on where we are at in each phase of managing the lead. Each member of the team, in reviewing the progress report, should identify their priorities in relation to the goals or weekly activities. Once discussed at the weekly progress meeting, they are recorded on the "to do" list by each individual person for completion.

A final word of caution...Make sure you've got the right person to act as the Prospector. In the A/E/C industry, there are many wonderful and truly talented people with "technical skills." You know these people intimately. They hold positions as architects, engineers and contractors.

The challenge is to attract and create meaningful work for people with personality traits that may be different from that of the core operational or technical talent. For the role of Prospector, companies need to find individuals that can fit into their companies' culture while working effectively with the Rainmaker and Technical Expert.

Who is this person? When considering someone for the Prospector position, have an open mind. Having trained many of these people, they may be young, right out of college looking for their first "real" job- or they may be a former pharmaceutical rep who now wants a flexible part time job because they've opted to be a "stay-at-home mom." They may an unusual operations guy who happens to have an outgoing personality and the technical skills typically associated with "the technical expert."

If you are a small firm, you, the Principal may need to act more assertively in the Prospector role until you have the funds to delegate the responsibility and hire a full time person to fill the position. (You know this because if you are a small firm, this is your reality.) Instead of accepting this reality, I encourage you to prioritize replacing yourself with someone designated to the Prospector role. This way you'll have a system in place to assure sustainable growth.

If you are part of an established team, one person may come to mind as the right personality for the Prospector role. Either way, the important thing is that someone with the critical communication, documentation and relationship initiation skills step up to the plate. When I describe this person to firms considering hiring for the role, I frequently use the description of "Rush Chairman" because it fits so well this personality type. They are friendly, comfortable with new people and generally really enjoy socializing and networking. It comes so natural to them, that they just tend to ooze bubbly charisma that attracts others. You know these people, they tend to have a positive personal demeanor and when in a hospitable climate are the life of a party.

What happens when the wrong person assumes the Prospector role? It's really quite simple. Very little. If you examine the results of the sales efforts for the team, should you get the wrong person in the Prospecting role, the result will be few or no new qualified leads.

In one instance, during the national pilot program for this new sales methodology, I was asked to train a team that included an individual the President felt would be appropriate to be the Prospector.

Once I arrived to train this team and had some time with the key players, I was really concerned about the individual that they had designated to act as Prospector. You see, the person they had asked to act as the Prospector really wasn't a Prospector personality. In fact, at best he was wired for marketing administration.

He had an extensive background in graphic art design and liked to spend most of his time working alone on proposal design or drafting, layouts and building renderings. He liked to be alone at the drafting table or computer. (The key word here is "alone".) He said he wanted to act as Prospector, and I think when he knew I had been hired to introduce the team to a new sales process; on some level, he knew his job depended on it. So he tried.

However, when we went into training and talked about walking into businesses at industrial and manufacturing parks surrounding work sites, he was the first to voice a long list of concerns. He just didn't see why we needed to make the effort.

I then evaluated carefully his body language during the training. He crossed his arms, was quiet and avoided interacting with the group on training or skill development exercises. When asked, he had many concerns why he felt this program "just wasn't going to work."

The truth was, we were asking him to do things he really wasn't comfortable with– and as I walked with the company President to the airport terminal, I candidly told him that I had deep concerns about the person that they'd asked to act as Prospector.

In retrospect, he made it working for the company for one more year before they let him go. This was a sad waste of time and opportunity for the contractor, and we knew as early as the training session that the candidate did not feel *comfortable with the role he would perform.* ***Don't let this*** ***happen to you****!*

As you take stock of the skill sets on your team and consider what it might take to "accommodate" certain people that you are currently committed to, don't underestimate the importance of the role of Prospector. The company that I just mentioned let a precious year go by where they went from $100 million in annual revenue to $58 million in revenue. Their revenue dipped for many reasons, not for this reason alone, however, not having the right person in the Prospecting role certainly did not help.

The Prospector Job Description
The following is a job description you might use in filling the CRD or Prospector role:

-Job Posting-
Usual introductory stuff about the company, the industry, etc....

Our ideal candidate has experience in business- to- business communications and/or sales. ***They demonstrate an enthusiasm to meet*** ***new people and have a desire to participate in a structured sales process.*** *A background in communications, sales management or marketing is preferred, but not required. Team training, ongoing coaching and mentoring will be provided for the right candidate. Starting salary is negotiable based on level of experience.*

Job Description: Community Relations Director
The Community Relations Director (CRD) is responsible for outbound prospecting efforts (day- to- day sales efforts) associated with our marketing plan. This role is critical to identifying viable prospects and associated new business opportunities. As the ambassador for Acme Contracting, this person must possess great communication and documentation skills. They will make initial contact with prospects, collect key information and manage the information through our sales process. Advancement opportunities will be associated with demonstrated knowledge of the construction industry and the ability to contribute to the sales process past initial prospecting.

The Community Relations Director:

- *Is first and foremost a solution provider for potential new customers of our company, and functions as an ambassador for new business contacts*
- *Collects and organizes prospect information*
- *Plans, initiates and manages all outbound efforts associated with prospecting*
- *Monitors daily and weekly personal progress, striving to achieve production benchmarks associated with daily prospecting activities*
- *Maintains a strategic 12-month plan for the sales team*
- *Responds to ongoing management coaching and professional development*

Required Skills:

- *Is a "self-starter," someone who feels comfortable meeting people and initiating communication, has an interest or demonstrated ability in the area of sales; recognizes the value of being a business solutions provider, as opposed to pushing a product*
- *Has the ability to work independently and adhere to process*
- *Demonstrates follow-through abilities, taking a project through several specific steps and enjoys process*
- ***Has patience****. The long sales process associated with developing and managing the customer relationship requires patience as the customer development process can be as long as 12 to 24 months.*
- ***Desires critique, feedback and development associated with personal presentation skills****. Demonstrates a familiarity with industry terminology and a willingness to learn the intricacies associated with the general construction processes. We seek evidence of this within 3 months of training or hire.*
- *Demonstrates increasing skills and willingness to learn more comprehensive information about the construction industry as a whole and our firm -within 6 to 12 months of initial training or hire*
- *Wants to be held accountable for performance, feels comfortable with processes designed to document and measure levels of ability*
- *Has familiarity with common computer software programs (such as Microsoft Word and Excel), can use e-mail and is comfortable with document formatting*

What can you expect of a Prospector?

There are several answers to adequately address this question. First, after much research, I can tell you with confidence that a Prospector will only perform to the level at which they are supported by the rest of the Executive team. Let me elaborate on this issue. If the Prospector is brought on, provided training (this book or a training course), and then is turned loose to perform without true accountability for daily or weekly performance from his team, then only limited results will be obtained.

For solid and sustainable results to be achieved, a Prospector has got to feel the support and dedication of his entire team from the top of the company on down. There must be weekly progress meetings, accessibility to key executive individuals supporting qualification efforts, and meaningful dialog about the direction of the marketing plan in relation to the daily activities associated with the sales team. If the Prospector is constantly filling the pipeline with viable leads that fail to be properly qualified and closed, the situation can become very disappointing for the Prospector. When the team wins, everybody has got to taste the victory, that's why it's important to consider adequate compensation bonuses (incentives) for sales leads or new business that convert to top-line revenue for the company.

Although the goal for the entire team is the conversion of Blues to Reds, the Prospector ought to have proper incentives to fill the pipeline with qualified Yellows and Blues.

Another key consideration in terms of team performance is that the Closer or current "Rainmaker" will only relinquish control to the team in proportion to their level of confidence that the teams can follow the system presented. Should the team have issues with adhering to process, or balk at being held accountable, the team members will find it increasingly difficult to succeed in their roles, as the old "Rainmaker" will be back at the helm in the center of everything. In other words, everybody has to take the initial leap of faith this system requires and "Just Do It" (as Nike so eloquently put it).

Here's the detailed punch list you need to get started. Are you ready for the self-quiz? Don't cheat.

Phase 1: Lead Generation Checklist

<u>C</u>ommunication: *What are we communicating internally to our team? Externally to prospects?*

Internal:
- ☐ *Decide who will be responsible to act as Prospector, Technical Expert and Closer*
- ☐ *Create the MAP™ and develop each team member's short-term plans.*
- ☐ *Review current list of prospects, assign them into categories of Yellow, Blue and Red based on descriptions provided.*
- ☐ *Set and confirm the first date for progress reporting.*
- ☐ *Review logos, brand, website and worksite signage. Is it consistent? Interesting? Producing inquiries or comments? Make a decision and do something about it if it's not.*

External:
- ☐ *Begin contact with prioritized targets in the section "What We Know."*
- ☐ *Begin contact with prioritized targets in the section "What We Don't Know."*
- ☐ *Seek introduction to the Decision Maker, and document details of what you learn.*
- ☐ *Categorize resulting leads as Yellow, Blue and Red on the progress report.*

<u>O</u>rganization: *How are we organizing the team? Its resources?*

- ☐ *Use your company calendar to indicate when prospecting activities will occur, if the Prospector plans to be out of the office. The Technical Expert should also let the Prospector know of availability to help qualify leads.*

☐ *Double check supplies (such as business cards, case studies, clipboard with paper and pens) before you head out the door for prospecting activities.*

Documentation: *How do we document progress?*

☐ *Update the progress report.*
☐ *Update the weekly to-do lists.*
☐ *On a monthly basis, update short-term plans and review progress to the goals indicated on the MAP ™.*
☐ *Every six months, update the MAP ™.*

Evaluation: *How do we evaluate performance?*

Assuming the Prospector invests 28 hours per week in a metro market comparable to that of Kansas City (population 2MM), the results should be as follows:

☐ *3 days a week, 4 hours per day in the field, making walk-in or outbound calls to prospects, additional time is factored in for travel (3 hours).*
☐ *Assumes 4 attempts per hour, 16 attempts per day or 48 per week.*
☐ *50% of efforts will result in a disqualified attempt (or dead end).*
☐ *50% will be productive, resulting in 18 Yellows, 5 Blues and 1 Red = 24 total leads per week.*

Should the market be rural or smaller, the results will be proportionate to the size of market. For example in North Dakota, we shoot for 2 Yellows, 1 Blue or 1 Red -as the leads are simply harder to come across.

Discussion Questions for the team:

Does everyone understand the purpose of the MAP™ and the short-term plans?

Who will be the Prospector? Based on the description of the job responsibilities, is there a good match between the person selected and the type of work they will be responsible for?

What are the top three things that could be problematic for the team? What can you do now to overcome these issues?

What factors make you think that change is necessary for your organization? What do you as a member of the team hope to contribute? What do you as a team hope to achieve?

Test Your Knowledge:

Name the 3 members of the sales team by title:

Briefly describe the role of the Prospector. What they are responsible for? Why are they so important?

What is a MAP™? What are the two sections of the MAP™?

What is "proactive prospecting"? Why is it important?

What is a Yellow lead, a Blue lead, a Red lead?

Who is responsible for updating the weekly progress report? The to-do list?

Why should the team be held accountable to hold weekly progress meetings?

What two pieces of paper should be at the weekly progress meetings?

Chapter Five

Whoa! Slow down....
It's time for Phase 2: Lead Qualification

Assuming you've now generated some solid leads, the goal is to keep them moving in your pipeline. You've got Yellow leads that need to move to Blue, and Blue leads that need to go to Red. Let's begin with the Yellow leads.

Yellow to Blue

If you've properly categorized the prospect as Yellow, you need more information to learn what this company may be doing and when. This is typically handled by the Prospector, who spends time calling back new contacts to learn more about opportunities associated with activity that's been indicated.

During this initial qualification, the Prospector asks these questions:
- How long has your company been in business?
- Have you thought about building or been through renovations before?
- What is contributing to the need for new space requirements?
- What is the satisfaction with your location? Facilities?
- What's the motivation for building? Timeline?
- Who is the decision maker?

Once the lead is <u>confirmed to be doing something</u> ***and*** has <u>indicated a willingness to meet</u> with the Prospector to discuss the situation, the lead is classified as a Blue, and the Technical Expert is notified of the pending meeting. At this point, the goal is to really slow things down, which may sound nuts- but it is very important. The primary reason that you need to slow down is straightforward: no one writes a million dollar check to a company or person they hardly know. And getting to know someone takes time, real honest-to-goodness time. So the purpose of Phase 2 is to create reasons to have multiple meetings, to ensure that you have time to learn the details of their situation and earn their trust.

Keep in mind that your priorities directly compete with those of the prospect. From the prospect's point of view, they see you as a free consultant who, when it comes down to details, can afford to compete on price. They have two goals - only two, so make sure you catch this. **Their first goal is to get you to provide as much detail as they can get you to provide for free. Their second goal is to get from you a price**.

Your goals are clearly different from theirs. You want to learn the details of their situation, which requires disclosure and trust. You want to eliminate the competition and have them develop a loyalty to you, which requires respect for your unique solution. And finally, you want to understand how they will make their decision. This requires an understanding of where they are on the education or assumption curve.

When you provide a proposal, will they understand what determines the bottom-line price? If they compare proposals, will they recognize the differences? Have you answered all of the critical questions to make sure that, by the time you put your estimating team to the task, all the tough questions have been answered so that there are few surprises? Lead qualification is all about reducing risks by creating structured time with the prospect, before you go through the drill of investing further precious time and resources.

The Two Types of Prospects

As I mentioned earlier, there are only two types of prospects: those who have bought services like yours before, and those that have not. Both require a delicate approach. For the prospect that has never bought services like yours before, it's all about education. Your goal is to help them understand all of the issues that require their thoughtful consideration as they determine the best approach for their situation. Simply said, they have <u>no idea</u> what is involved and most likely would vastly underestimate what is required.

From site selection, soil testing to permits, to construction approach or financing...these prospects have usually no idea what is required in terms of decisions that must be made for them to hit their goal of building in 12 to 18 months. Your primary goal in working with an inexperienced Blue prospect is to understand where they are at on the education curve, and to "fill the gaps" with meetings designed to educate them, giving them confidence that you are the strategic solution provider. View it as a transaction. You provide them important information, while they in turn provide you with valuable time with the decision maker. As long as your expectations of disclosure and honesty about your requirements to keep moving forward are met, this is a reasonable exchange.

The other type of prospect is the experienced prospect or someone who has bought products and services like yours before. They may have had a good experience, or they may have had a negative experience...but the point is that they have had some type of experience which is unique to their frame of reference. **Your goal in the initial meetings with this type of prospect is to understand what happened, how they felt about it, and what they hope may be different in dealing with your company.** With this type of prospect, you may run into two key attitudes: (1) a degree of cynicism, as they think they "know it all," or (2) a degree of fear; they need information or reassurance to overcome the "pain" of a past experience.

Two types of prospects, both of which require careful communication to establish a purpose and direction for the "process" of education or assumption management that you will take them through.

Set the Stage
In the initial meetings with Blues, it's critical to communicate precisely what your intentions are. Meetings should always revolve around an established agenda. The meetings should rarely if ever take longer than an hour, and you should always provide an agenda in advance to lay out on the table what you hope to cover. Your goal is two-fold. First, you want to provide them knowledge or information to help them continue to make decisions. Second, you need to always prepare them for what they should expect next, so that you can meet and exceed their expectations. I wish this were as simple as it sounds.

Starting the Dialog to Establish Trust & Disclosure
As you begin meeting with prospects, your goal is to educate them or to understand more about their assumptions "doing business with you." **At each point of interaction, you let them know why you're in contact, and you let them know upfront if they decide it's not an appropriate match, you expect them to they tell you so.** With each meeting, you give the prospect permission to say, "I'm not moving forward," "I'm not interested," or "you are not the right vendor for my needs."

WHY WOULD YOU DO THIS? You are in sales, and this sounds like an insane tactic to use with a prospect. You do this for several reasons, but the primary reason is to disarm them.

If they think you are trying to sell something, the best thing to do is to tell them you are not trying to sell them something. That in fact, your company partners with its clients and understands that in pursuing construction, choosing a contractor is a tremendous decision. Who they choose to entrust with their company's single largest investment is a very critical decision, and not something to be taken lightly. So if it's not a good match, you really understand and want to know at the earliest possible time. You tell them that you are absolutely fine with it not being a perfect match, which causes them to exhale that breath they've been holding...and feel much less suspicious about your intentions. Now that the elephant is out of the room, you can take one of two routes: educate the inexperienced prospect, or re-educate the experienced prospect.

The Eight Critical Questions
So you know they are doing something, and it's time to weave the eight key questions into the educational or re-educational process. Let's look at each question and examine why it's important. Keep in mind that as you review the questions, they are listed here starting with the most valuable - not the order in which you should ask them.

What is the timeline for the project?
This is obvious and easy. If the timeline isn't clear, then it's safe to assume that the prospect may not be serious about moving forward. The more specific the answer to this question, the more likely that the prospect will purchase services of some kind. If you are dealing with an inexperienced prospect, they may have a completely unrealistic view on this issue. They may think that they can get something built in very short order, having no idea what decisions must be made. When the prospect answers this question, you need to be careful to note any caveats

they mention that may cause the timeline to expand or contract.

What is the budget? What are the assumptions about price? How do they define "value"? Is the financing in place?

This is a loaded and multi-faceted question that addresses how the prospect views price vs. perceived value. For an inexperienced prospect, they may have no idea how to establish a budget- or may have a simple view of how a budget is determined, such as price per square foot. For an experienced prospect, the issue of how they define value will greatly relate to their prior experience in dealing with and perhaps financing the building process. If they had a difficult experience with change orders, or had trouble on any other facet of the job, you can be relatively sure the experience re-defined the issue of value in their mind. Normally, the issue of financing, planned budget or perceived value tends to surface only after there has been significant face time with the decision maker and you've had time to really establish your approach to creating a proposal, which includes the pricing estimate. If you've done a proper job from the beginning of setting the tone for disclosure and being upfront with details, addressing this issue becomes easier.

Who is the Decision Maker?

Often when working with a group (church committees, medical/ healthcare administrators, and agricultural co-ops, for example) it can be difficult to identify "the Decision Maker"- the person with the power to make a decision on a proposal. What can be especially tricky is when there is a committee that makes the decision, or in a new development situation, a group of investors. As the Closer can attest, sometimes the Decision Maker hides in a pack of other people, trying to mask their identity until after a decision is announced. A seasoned Closer knows that there are several signs of who the true Decision Maker is. Here are some quick tips to help you ferret out who is in control when it's not readily obvious:

- Identify the person in the group that other people tend to concede with or seek the approval of. By the type of questions being asked, who does everyone seem to shift towards (in terms of body language) or who is the last in the group to ask questions. Careful observation of how the group tends to communicate or interact as a whole will tend to finger-point to the leader.
- Who comes in late to meetings, takes few notes- and will also abruptly leave at times?
- Who likes to talk about vision, opportunity or the investment, core assumptions behind the business plan?

What guidelines will they use to select a contractor partner in review of the proposal?
Right up there with the discussion on budget, this ranks as a critical consideration. It's this question, if carefully asked and timed, which can reveal a prospect that is misleading you in the area of budget, or price vs. value. For example, if in discussing the budget the focus of the discussion centers on the notion of **quality**, and they answer that **price** will be the driving factor in the contractor selected, it should be a solid indicator that you need further clarification on how their definition of value (not yours) relates to price before a proposal is provided. If their definition of value has been stated, and the criteria they will use to select a contractor has been clearly described- it should be obvious how best to approach the formatting and components of a winning proposal.

Who is the competition? What is their history with the prospect?
A tough question but worth asking, particularly if there's a known history with another vendor. A best example that I can provide on this happened with a client that was asked

by an Architect to bid a high-rise, multi-tenant living facility. This Architect had a history of doing business with a very competitive contractor, so my client was baffled when the Architect asked to meet with them under the guise that this might "finally be the opportunity" for them to do some work together. Instead of asking the Architect what role this other competitor might have and addressing the tough question straight up, they just went along with the Architect under the impression that to ask might jeopardize the "well intended" politics of the new opportunity. Well, you can guess exactly what happened. The other contractor caught wind of the deal and came in with an competing proposal at the last minute. Since the issue of the competitor hadn't been fully addressed, the Architect said that he'd made a last-minute decision to go with the lesser "bid"– from his buddy; my client lost a million-dollar-plus deal over $90K - which was ridiculous.

Had my client addressed this issue of who is the competition and what will their role be if we move forward, it would have at least made the selection of the other proposal more uncomfortable for the Architect- and would have saved my client the time and the trouble of estimating a job they were "being shopped" for (as the client, in this case the Architect, only was looking to obtain an alternate set of numbers to satisfy their client). My client was furious when this happened, so I advise you to ask the tough question early. Not to say that the answer will always be honest - but at least you can comfort yourself in that you did everything possible to avoid this becoming a last-minute, "pop-up" issue.

As an interesting footnote: for his next prospect meeting, my client wrote up a simple case study describing how they lost an anonymous million dollar deal over a negotiable $90K. He then used this case study to set up the explanation of his approach to disclosure issues with the new prospect. He said

100

upfront, if it's not a "right fit," it's ok. This company would much rather identify "upfront" the key issues, so that they could avoid last-minute losses.

<u>Have we addressed the proprietary nature of the solution we will provide?</u>
Too frequently, in a rush to put a proposal on the table, the A/E/C contractor fails to describe the value of the proprietary approach to the project that they have uniquely chosen. They fail to ask that the information be considered their intellectual property. Instead, what was a brilliant recommendation for a heating and AC airflow issue for a manufacturing plant gets rolled carelessly into a conversation with a key competitor. I can't be too strong here so here I go...**PROTECT YOURSELF**! Often I'm asked by my clients during training *"Does a non-disclosure document really work? Does it make the prospect think you don't trust them? Is the subject worth addressing?"* Well, you tell me, based on your experience with the issue.

If it does work, then you are protected. If it doesn't work, then it's safe to assume that the prospect was going to do the dirty deed anyway- so you've taken a common business means to protect yourself. You may choose not to pursue that protection, but at least you've made known to the prospect that you've provided value in your approach to solving their problems...and you expect this value to be respected. Please, protect your intellectual property (your proposal) from being shopped to your competitors. It's up to you to pick the time to address this, but the earlier the better in the Blue qualification process. As I conclude my sermon, if the industry as a whole would take a unified view of this issue, it would be a moot point and not be on this list; as for other industries, it's standard procedure to protect the content and approach associated with your proposal. Enough said.

What is the timeline for a decision to be made once the proposal is submitted?

This seems like the dumb question on the list, but again- you'd be amazed how many times truly seasoned Closers fail to ask this and get dragged around for months by prospects not willing to make the decision. By asking the question and making sure your prospect has seen you record their answer, the follow-up question is, "May I call you on (date) to visit with you about your decision?" Nail them down on a timeline so that you know what to expect on when a decision will be made. Again, last-minute financing issues might throw this out the window…but in asking the question, you've outlined the approach that they must contend with in your effort to close the deal.

What are our next steps to move the client through the pipeline, or take them out? What is the agenda for the next client meeting?

This question is all about you. What do you want next from the prospect based on the information they've provided? What areas do you need to further clarify? What key questions have yet to be asked? What assumptions have you not yet addressed? Throughout the entire sales process, you are in control and your intellectual property should be protected at every step of disclosure. You should be assessing the prospect, identifying their educational needs, their core assumptions about what the next step should be in their opinion, and you should be *aggressively managing their expectations* so that there are no surprises.

In their mind, you should be the *expert.* You should be the kind person who graciously comes in well prepared for each meeting. You need to be perceived as the company readily sharing solutions, but smart enough in business to use common tools to protect the solutions you propose. And most importantly, you need to be the honest soul who

102

tells them from day one that this is a process that requires trust and disclosure so that their needs can be identified and met. You only want to provide for them what "it" is they want for themselves. It's up to you to establish their trust and respect so that you can draw out of them over the course of several meetings exactly what "that" is. When you do, it's a win/win. When you hit a wall and sense you aren't being afforded the kindness of disclosure in an effort to meet their needs, then you've got the power to determine where they fall in terms of internal priorities and the time you plan on investing in their request for an estimate, proposal or "bid".

PPC Selling
When I conduct training on the qualification process, I address something I refer to as PPC selling. PPC stands for the following acronym: Proprietary Solution, Price and Competition. I believe it is important to address these things in the early phases of relationship development with a prospect. I've found in reviewing these classic three "sticky wickets" of sales, that way too often these issues are left unaddressed with the prospect until they become a problem. Much like an iceberg, they look like small issues on the surface...but when left unattended, they can dramatically change your ability to close the deal if you hit one. The most important thing to keep in mind in terms of timing is that when you are in the early phases of relationship development, it's best to lay your cards on the table about how you do things and why.

Most people tend to avoid these hard subjects in an effort to "win" the **favor** of the prospect- when in reality the **respect** of the prospect is a far more important virtue to shoot for in terms of getting the deal done. The longer these issues are unaddressed in the qualifying process (Phase 2), the more difficult they become to address as the dialog continues over time. Trust me; it's easier to ask these tough questions in the beginning as it sets the tone for the communication to be one of extreme honesty, which only helps to create credibility with the prospect. If you respect yourself, they will too.

Who is responsible for managing the Blue lead?
The answer to this question really depends on experience, with regards to the Prospector. If they are young and new to the role, then they need to attend qualification meetings for the Blue prospects with the Technical Expert, who can better sense the best time to ask the eight key questions while providing educational value for the prospect.

On the other hand, should the Prospector be somewhat seasoned, then they may go for quite a few rounds with the prospect before calling in the Technical Expert. It is important for the group to discuss in weekly meetings each of the eight key questions as they relate to the prospect, so that a proper agenda can be formulated with the right people in attendance for the next meeting.

The Prospector needs to know that at any time they can call upon the Technical Expert to attend an upcoming meeting with the prospect, so they can educate the client and present approaches to technical issues. It should be noted that if at any time the Blue lead begins to balk at further meetings and has not indicated a request for proposal date, then they can be bounced back to a Yellow classification, so that they do not continue to be classified as a Blue in the sales pipeline.

Of course, the nearer the prospect comes to requesting a proposal, the more important it is that the Prospector and Technical Expert ask the Closer to attend a meeting to further take the Blue to a Red.

NO MORE BIDS!

Bids vs. Estimates vs. Proposals...
Your choice of terms REALLY matters!

On a final "qualifying" note, does your company use the word "bid" to describe an estimate or a proposal? If so...**PLEASE STOP IT NOW**. Although the industry has a history of "hard bid" procurement methods, and it may be your natural word of choice, this term has **no place in your pursuit of negotiated or design-build work**. I mean absolutely **no place** in your discussions with prospects or strategic partners.

Why should you banish this word? Here's exactly why you must stop using this word right now:

> If you use the word "bid," you immediately assume competition. Just the choice of the word alone assumes you are "bidding against something or someone."

If you use the word, it immediately commoditizes the solution you present. This word makes the entire scope of what you've proposed come down to a number- which is precisely what you want to avoid.

And finally, when someone "bids" for something, it tends to indicate a willingness to negotiate. Why would you set the stage for a negotiated deal in these terms? There is no reason I can think of.

Using this term is a terrible choice that runs counter to every bit of value and differentiation that you are working to establish in the mind of the prospect. When talking to the client about a proposal or estimate, that's what it is. Why is it when you receive an estimate for carpet cleaning at your home residence, you safely assume that the number they give you is what you will pay for the service? Why isn't this true for your industry?

I'll tell you why. Seldom does the contractor invest the time required in the qualification process to properly position the value of the proposal or estimate in the mind of the client. They rush to get a number or bid on the table in an effort to be perceived as "responsive." In doing so, they don't slow down enough to carefully analyze what the client is really asking for, and they certainly haven't identified what the client will require to make a decision. Too often, the client doesn't even know what they really want or can afford. How can you help them if you haven't spent time with them to define the scope and financial commitments required of their request?

If they don't know the right questions to ask, there's no way they can recognize the value of the answer you provide. Are you getting this? Think about it. And remember:

NO MORE BIDS!

I have seen the difference this can make with my clients. Generally, they have been able to greatly reduce the percentage of bid work and greatly increase the amount of negotiated work. One client went from 100% competitive low-margin hard bid work to 90% negotiated high-margin work by following the CODE program. When I first met with the owner, he explained that his clients always required competitive bids and there was no way to avoid the bidding process in his market. He was frustrated and felt as if the situation were hopeless. It took about a year for the changes to switch the situation around. Imagine the difference to his attitude and to his bottom line after his change in strategy! The impact was profound!

In Phase 2, it's all about presenting a structured educational process to the client, one that's designed to take the guesswork out the proposal you'll design. If you've done your job effectively in Phase 2, the prospect will know exactly why each part of the proposal is there.

You'll have effectively managed their expectations through each meeting– which results in a sales process that should run without surprises. You have effectively positioned your firm to close the deal as you transition the Blue prospect to a Red in **Phase 3: The Sales Pitch**.

Phase 2: Lead Qualification Checklist

Communication: *What are we communicating internally to our team? Externally to prospects?*

Internal:
- ☐ Decide who will be responsible to continue to qualify each lead and what the agenda should be for each upcoming meeting.
- ☐ Review the eight critical questions associated with each Blue lead to separate "what you know and have confirmed" from "what you assume to be true."
- ☐ Review your current list of Yellow prospects; schedule call-backs for further qualification.
- ☐ Confirm with your team all pending Blue meetings and determine who on the team is best suited and available to attend and what other outside resources or partners might be appropriate to bring to the table.
- ☐ As the prospect gets close to identifying a request for proposal date, alert the estimating team as early as possible so they can properly plan.

External:
- ☐ Confirm with the prospect their level of experience, if they are new to the construction process or not.
- ☐ Identify the issues of greatest concern to the prospect and set meetings to address these concerns.
- ☐ Seek introduction to the Decision Maker and document what you learn, making sure to clarify any details you are not clear on.

Organization: *How are we organizing the team? Its resources?*

- ☐ *Use your company calendar to indicate when qualification meetings will occur so that appropriate team members schedule their time accordingly.*
- ☐ *Determine who is managing the lead at all times and who will communicate with the prospect after each meeting.*

Documentation*: How do we document progress?*

- ☐ *Update the progress report as Yellows move to Blues, and Blues move to Reds. Blue lead management takes priority over Yellow; Red lead management takes priority over Blue.*
- ☐ *Continue to document prospect answers to the eight key questions to document where you are in the process of qualifying Yellow and Blue leads. Enter it into your company sales database if one is available.*

Evaluation: *How do we evaluate performance?*

- ☐ *Weekly, it's all about keeping the pipeline filled and moving. Regularly review: how many Yellows have become Blues? How many Blues are moving toward requesting a proposal and transitioning to Reds?*
- ☐ *Be sensitive to a developing hole in the pipeline. A Blue hole is a bad thing. To avoid this, keep the numbers of prospects in the pipeline as evenly spread as possible through the Yellows and Blues.*
- ☐ *For a mid-sized construction firm ($50MM-$300MM in revenue), an ideal pipeline progress report would feature 20-30 total prospects: 15 Yellows, 10 Blues and 5 Reds would be ideal from a management standpoint. Keep an eye on the numbers of prospects in each category, and then compare the job start dates to calendars divided by quarters. This should greatly help you identify operational capacity concerns.*

Discussion Questions for the team:

Does everyone understand the purpose of intentionally slowing things down in Phase 2: Lead Qualification?

As a team, do we have a history of asking the eight key questions? If not, why? What keeps us from asking these questions?

How will the Prospector know when to call in the Technical Expert? Have they received enough feedback from the team so that the expectation is clear when the Technical Expert should be involved?

Think of the eight questions. As a team reminisce about the times that you've lost or gained business based on how you handled these key questions. Tell war stories about your experience and be honest.

Do you agree that there are only two types of prospects? What's been your experience or opinion on the issue of how to handle prospects? How does this impact the approach you take with prospects, and the role you will play with others on the team?

Test Your Knowledge:

Describe generally which members of the team are active in Phase 2.

Describe the two types of prospects you work with in Phase 2.

To the best of your memory, try to re-call the eight key questions.

What transaction is happening in qualifying the lead? Hint: You are providing valuable education and resources, and the prospect is providing _____.

Why should you have an agenda for each prospect meeting?

Why should you describe to the prospect your approach to the process they will go through? Why manage their expectations?

When does a Blue lead become a Red?

Chapter Seven

Hallelujah. It's Phase 3:
The Sales Pitch

OK. We generated the lead in Phase 1. We qualified the lead in Phase 2. Now, is the moment we've all been waiting for...the actual "sales pitch." This is when the Blue lead has asked that a proposal be developed. They've indicated a date in which they want to see a proposal. The date has been set, so they've officially transitioned from Blue to Red. Wow, a very nice, big moment. By this time, all eight key questions should be answered, or at a minimum should have been asked.

You should know their budget, their concerns about price, notions of value and any pending competition that might spring out of the woodwork at the last minute. In other words, you should be perfectly positioned to close the deal.

If you've built a good foundation, then you should be prepared to submit a winning proposal. At this point, it's a matter of formalities and finalizing the deal. What do you need to focus on at this point? It's simple. Let's start with preparing to succeed.

No surprises and no fire drills.
By the time you've properly taken a Yellow to Blue, and a Blue to Red, it should be clear that the process is in motion and the prospect is moving closer to requesting a proposal. If the team is being regularly updated, it should not come as a surprise when the date is selected. What this translates to in terms of internal preparation is that there's a potential date on the horizon based on suggested timelines for the project to start - so we should prepare accordingly. If

things are "done properly," there really should be no last minute drills that catch everyone off balance and unprepared. In a perfect world, this is how it works...But it's not a perfect world. So what types of issues should be addressed when preparing for proposal development?

Use of templates is key to simplifying document production.
What sections of your proposals are the same in every proposal you write? What sections are customized? After working with many companies that all face the same requirements; I typically see eight sections in every proposal, five of which are usually customized for the project.

Customized sections typically include:
- Clarifications: Assumptions of the estimator.
- Team: An organization chart with names, titles and biographies of the management team.
- Schedule: Technical aspects of site management and associated deadlines.
- Costs: Estimated project costs.
- Response: Covers the approach to the project, identifying the key issues or "pain" that the approach must overcome for the prospect.

Standardized, or non-customized, templates sections of the proposal typically include:
- Company General Information/ Financial Statements / Proof of Bonding Capacity: Description of the company, its history, safety standards and financial capacity to assume risk.
- Projects: Case studies of similar projects, photos and testimonials from satisfied customers.
- References: Testimonials from core customers with contact information.

I realize it may sound elementary to cover this, but you'd be shocked how many companies struggle to find the electronic documents that they use all the time. If you are one of these companies, one of the most important things you can do is to get aggressive about organizing your electronic files so that information is really at your fingertips. In one situation with a company spanning three generations, I was shocked to learn on a $23 million proposal that we were scrambling to provide case study details on similar projects. There's no reason for this; one day spent organizing electronic files can eliminate this pain.

Preparing for the Final Pitch

Beyond preparation of the physical proposal document, there are other core elements to consider, such as the cover letter, and how to approach the prospect's review of the proposal document (the presentation). By this time, the prospect should be familiar with the Closer and should have had some face time to establish rapport. The Closer or Technical Expert (in some cases the Estimator) should be prepared to review in detail at the presentation the core issues associated with price and project start-up, using the answers to the eight key questions to close the deal. Most importantly, **the Closer needs to review in detail all the assumptions or core concerns that have been shared by the prospect and summarize clearly how these issues have been resolved in the proposal presented**. You have this key opportunity to tell them what you've heard, show them how you've solved their problem, and ask for the business.

You don't want to mess this up considering all the work you've invested to this point. So, if Murphy's Law says that if anything can go wrong, it probably will- how do you prepare like there's nothing like prayer and pray like there's nothing like preparation? Get prepared for anything. What am I talking about?

Run a full dress rehearsal and strategy session. Take the time to actually run through the big pitch in advance of the big pitch. Ask someone you trust to listen to your approach, glance through your materials and provide you feedback on what they see or hear. Talk to the team about what to wear. You would be shocked at the number of church committees I've interviewed that said the contractor that came in to pitch looking like they were headed to Harrah's Casino next. What specific details did they recall? Too many gold chains, taupe colored loafers, busy patterned acrylic sweaters with a tee-shirt showing underneath...Are you getting this picture? When you present at a church, dress like you are going to church. When you meet with a developer, look like an investor (very nice business casual). When you meet with an agricultural co-op, dress like one of the casual farm guys they feel comfortable doing business with. If it's a banker, dress in a white shirt and suit.

If you have any questions, ask your secretary, wife or significant other what to do. Too often the details are overlooked and what you are attempting to say is sadly lost in the sloppiness of what the prospect sees. Let me illustrate what I see clients doing to address this issue.

I have clients who are currently requiring the members of their sales team to do something unheard of in the industry.... Go as a group to Nordstrom for private fittings and counsel regarding wardrobe issues. Yes, you read that correctly. Not one, but actually several of my clients in an effort to annihilate the khaki-bland, often un-ironed world of Dockers that is the standard go to uniform for their employees has required their people to go in for a complete "sales pitch" wardrobe, complete with silk ties, Italian shoes and silk blend *slacks. This is a budgeted, planned priority for the team and is positioned as a group field trip. And wives, girlfriends or significant others are **not** invited to participate.*

As my mother says, "Shoes never lie." Before you even look down, ask yourself: What do the shoes you are wearing say about you?

Be prepared to pitch at their office, your office or any place in-between. Again, this may sound elementary but you'd be amazed how many meetings originally scheduled at a neutral location can be moved at the last minute for one reason or another. In one instance we had a few days' notice that an out-of-town developer was coming in for an office tour, which sent our team scrambling just to clean the conference area...C'mon! Be prepared for the possibility that the client preparing to spend millions with you just may want to see your office. And don't be embarrassed if it's modest; instead, use your surroundings to further reinforce your story to the prospect. If you haven't spent a fortune on a new office, it says that you are thrifty and can create efficiencies. If you do have the new office, play up just the opposite. You are progressive and growing, show them how you created efficiencies in your own site design.

Be prepared to be completely flexible with any last-minute client requests. Don't ever design a presentation approach that cannot be completely changed on the fly. High-tech or low-tech– be prepared to pitch without your slide show or any plug-in accessories should you find yourself in unusual circumstances. I have actually heard of prospects strategizing about how they plan to eliminate proposals from some competing firms by stating very specific requirements in the presentation room set-up and orientation, with the intention of telling pitch teams moments before they walk in that they've changed their mind and now they've got new requirements for how the

116

room will be arranged. **They may really want to test you.** Can you be flexible under pressure? How will your team react? If you can demonstrate flexibility to the prospect at this juncture, it speaks credibly to your capability to handle any project changes as they move forward.

Use the cover letter strategically. Too many times, in a rush to get the proposal out the door, too little time is put into this document. This document should feature no more than three critical issues that your proposal will solve for the client and should prominently feature the bottom-line price. As the Closer will tell you, the first thing the prospect looks for in the proposal is the price. Save them the "flip to find it" effort and put it right front and center on the cover document. By this time, there should be no surprises, so tell them what they already know.

Always try to be last to present. A common strategy, but an important one. If you are the last of several competitors to pitch, you can ask the key questions, "How does my proposal stack up to the competition?" followed by the ever popular, "If all things were equal, what would cause you to select us over them?" If you can't be last, be first and set the bar at a steep height for others coming in after you.

When dealing with a "Red" prospect cattle call, <u>really</u> do your homework to differentiate yourself and your firm. Sometimes business moves very fast. You get a call out of the blue, the developer is flying in to meet you – and a deal is moving very quickly (a truly "on fire" Red prospect pops out of nowhere). When this happens, the process I've described just naturally compresses. The parameters are that you have a good shot with the prospect, but the competition is intense, and there's clearly a very short time frame (so you won't have the time to "slow things down" that's required in Phase 2).

When this happens (and in life you can count on the fact that it always does), you've got to think very strategically as a team. All too often, when the prospect is moving fast and initial interviews are happening quickly for a selection committee to narrow the field, the companies that come in **truly** prepared get a shot at the title.

In one situation, I had *visited* previously with a contractor that ended up being one of my core client's competitors. My client ended up being interviewed in a head-to-head competition with this other player for a pitch to land a very sweet negotiated deal. Since I knew a bit about the competition, I knew they had a problem with "really doing their homework" or preparing properly before the pitch.

I prepped my client extensively prior to the interview...and guess what? They easily took the business away from the other contractor because they did their homework (and a dress rehearsal) prior to meeting with the prospect. What constitutes basic homework? Review the prospect's website, corporate brochures or any information you can find. Search your local daily newspaper and local business journal websites for news articles too. Know their history, who leads the organization and how this project plays into their strategic vision. Get a roster of who will attend the interview, and try to determine each person's role in the selection process.

Remember that at any pre-qualifying "Red" interview, your goal should be to get them talking about themselves- not to talk too much about yourself and your firm. You are knowledgeable and experienced; otherwise, you wouldn't have been asked to attend in the first place. **Be confident of this: The prospect has done their homework and has invited you to make the short list because they know you are capable**. The purpose of the interview, whether it is stated or not, is to test one-on-one how knowledgeable you are, and to see if they like who you are as a person, and as a team. They want to determine the kind of value you bring to the table. They want to know what you can deliver- and how well you think on your feet.

You can address this unstated expectation by asking at the right time the compelling questions that create credibility and demonstrate your scope of experience. You must ask smart and timely questions to demonstrate what you know. What questions will you ask? Come up with the list before you walk in.

Never forget, the goal in dealing with a Red prospect is to get them talking about themselves. People do business with people they like. To get them to like you, they need to trust and respect you. To get them to trust and respect you, you need to ask questions that help them to recognize your value. These careful and pointed questions will greatly enhance your ability to get them to open up, which in turn will greatly enhance your opportunities to quickly establish rapport and a relationship with them.

Finally, in a Red interview, keep in mind that it's a lot like a negotiation. You've got to negotiate your way out of the line of competitors and squarely get in the front of the line. How can you do this quickly? **As a general rule, the person who talks less actually has more power or perceived influence.** When you meet with a Red prospect, ask yourself: Am I talking too much?

Phase 3: The Sales Pitch Checklist

Communication: *What are we communicating internally to our team? Externally to prospects?*

Internal:
- [ ] *Communicate to the team the proposal due date: confirm with estimating that all is moving forward.*
- [ ] *Review the eight critical questions associated with each Red lead to determine top priorities if operating in a short time frame.*
- [ ] *Review the need to have a prospect sign a non-disclosure agreement prior to proposal submission.*
- [ ] *Determine who will attend the sales presentation and select a date for a strategy session and dress rehearsal.*
- [ ] *Determine who is responsible for assembly of the physical proposal; identify resources they may need to access.*
- [ ] *Identify any missing details that estimating may be concerned about or any prospect research that has to be completed quickly to put the proposal together.*

External:
- [ ] *Confirm with the prospect the presentation date and who will be attending the meeting, and review the agenda.*

Organization: *How are we organizing the team? Its resources?*
- [ ] *Use your company calendar to indicate when the sales pitch will happen, coordinate all team members and estimating calendars.*
- [ ] *Conduct a strategy session and dress rehearsal.*

Documentation: *How do we document progress?*
- [ ] *Update the progress report as Blues identify proposal dates to become Reds.*

Evaluation: *How do we evaluate performance?*

☐ *How many Blues are moving toward requesting a proposal, and transitioning to Reds?*

☐ *Review how the Red lead "came to be." Did they go through our process? If not, how should we prioritize the questions we need to address in the little time we'll have with them before the proposal date?*

☐ *Review the eight key questions. Are you confident these questions have been answered? If any of the answers to the eight key questions are unclear, identify anything you can do to get clarification prior to the sales pitch.*

Discussion Questions for the team:

Does everyone know their role in the sales pitch? What role will estimating play in the actual sales pitch? Will they act as "Closer"?

How can we improve our preparation for a sales pitch? Do we normally have adequate preparation time?

Are we satisfied with the templates associated with our sales proposal? Could they be improved? If so, how?

When a request for a proposal comes in, do we have adequate time to respond? If not, why? What factors contribute to a "fire drill" atmosphere? How can these issues be avoided or addressed in the future?

Test Your Knowledge:

Describe generally which members of the team are active in Phase 3, the sales pitch.

When does the "sales pitch" officially begin?

What constitutes "doing your homework?"

What should you do if a truly quick-moving Red materializes out of nowhere?

Chapter Eight

Win or lose...What did we learn?
Phase 4: Post-Sales Activities

Debrief. Debrief. Debrief....sounds like a Hanes commercial, but it's not. It's the theme song for Phase 4 that focuses on post-sales activities. I want to pause to congratulate you at this point. You've been a faithful trooper, and you've made it through the rigors of a long sales process. Now I'm sure, you just want to sit back and relax. In your mind, at the end of a sales process, if you've turned the prospect into a client, you need to hurry on to address the million things associated with project start-up. Conversely, if you've lost a prospect, you're probably disappointed and are just really tired of thinking about it.

After a brutally long sales process, when you finally get to a decision from the client, you are just ready to move on. This is only natural. However, this impulse can undermine the long-term success and learning curve for your team. If you skip Phase 4 and just keep moving, you will miss a most important benefit to following a true process-driven sales approach –the chance for continual improvement. The reality you live in is that after an extremely intense sales effort, your team may be too busy, too tired or both to think about "another meeting." You may have very little energy or focus left. I recognize this. But at the end of the day, it's the perfect time to pause and consider what's happened and what you can do about it.

Phase 4: Post-sales begins when you've got a decision from the prospect. Once the decision is made, it needs to be communicated to the team in the form of a face-to-face meeting. This meeting is the great place to debrief. Too many times, when a company is disappointed about an outcome, a quiet email circulates to spread the bad news. Nobody really wants to talk about what happened, but the disappointment really stems from the desire to avoid mistakes or understand what happened so it can be addressed in future efforts. And when there's a big win, just the opposite happens. Everybody wants to talk about it, share the elephant-hunting story and rightly celebrate. So, given these realities – isn't it important to have a process designed to help the team decompress and learn?

The entire goal of the debriefing meeting is to review the process that you followed in managing the prospect from beginning to end so that you can determine if any critical steps were skipped. Questions discussed at the debriefing meeting might include:

- Was this a truly qualified prospect?
- Do we feel we "educated the client" and had adequate face time to create credibility and trust? Did we work from structured meeting agendas that accomplished our goals?
- Did we answer the eight key questions? Were our answers correct and complete, based on the outcome of the situation?
- Were we satisfied with the final proposal and supporting sales presentation? If not, why?
- Did we allow adequate time for the proposal to be produced? Did we prepare properly for the sales pitch?
- What are the general conclusions about why the project was won or lost? What can we learn from this experience as a team? How can you better support one another throughout the process?
- Did everyone fulfill the requirements of their role? Were communications clear?

If you've lost a prospect, at least keep the value of the relationship you've invested in. Yes, you did read that last sentence properly. Think about it for a moment. You've spent hours of face time with a prospect. You know them relatively well. Now, for whatever reason, you've lost the deal. For the most part, the disappointment would cause us to let go on some level. Don't. The prospect is still very valuable to you and your team. You have the golden opportunity to stay in touch with them, see how they are doing...and of course, to ask them for referrals. When you conclude a formal deal, open the door for the most important casual deal: the deal of friendship.

How do you turn a lost prospect into a friend?
Keep in touch. Start by sending them a thank-you note and a survey to ask them why they made the decision that they did.

Be a good-natured loser and offer to be a resource as they move forward. Choose to be one of the rare people that not only comes back to thank them for the kindness of their consideration but also extends a hand to them to help if they need anything as they move forward.

Let them know that you'll be in touch in the future. Stress that you really care about how their project goes and hope it goes well, even if they aren't working with you. In certain instances I've seen it happen where a competitor was selected, and because such positive post-sales relations were in place, the prospect came back to become a client on a much larger future project. Who knows, if the competitor can't handle the project, you will be the first company the client calls when something needs to change. Don't be short-sighted; be kind and know that the prospect will tell everyone about their experience, so why not make sure that what they say about your firm is outstanding?

126

Phase 4: Post-Sales Activity Checklist

Communication: *What are we communicating internally to our team? Externally to prospects?*

Internal:
- ☐ *Establish a date (as soon as possible) for a debrief meeting.*
- ☐ *Share the prospect's decision with the team at the meeting.*
- ☐ *Assign post-sales activity (writing the thank-you note and sending the survey) to the most appropriate team member.*
- ☐ *If a loss: Determine who on the team will keep in touch over time with the lost prospect.*
- ☐ *If a win: Get the project start-up team in place and engaged with start-up activities.*

External:
- ☐ *Confirm with the prospect their decision.*
- ☐ *Send thank you to the client.*
- ☐ *Send survey to the client; circulate to the team prior to the debriefing meeting.*

Organization: *How are we organizing the team? Its resources?*
- ☐ *Conduct the debriefing meeting.*

Documentation: *How do we document progress?*
- ☐ *Update the progress report as Reds make decisions; either convert to core customers or move out of the pipeline.*
- ☐ *Update your company scorecard of wins and losses, so you can stay motivated.*

Evaluation: _How do we evaluate performance?_

☐   _When a Red moves out of the pipeline, is another Yellow coming in? It's all about keeping the pipeline filled and moving. Even though it may be tempting when Reds are converting to revert away from finding new Yellows in the rush to manage the new business, beware. It's critical to keep filling the pipeline with Yellows; when Reds convert, the emphasis operationally can pull away from a focus on lead generation. Stay focused and replenish the pipeline._

☐   _Did we adhere to our process? Are we defining what we can do more effectively?_

☐   _What is our scorecard of wins to losses?_

Discussion Questions for the team:

Does everyone understand the importance of debriefing?

As a team, do we send a thank-you note and a post-sales customer survey? Do we assign someone to the lost prospect to continue communications?

Are we asking regularly how our process be improved? How our performance can be improved? How does this impact our internal performance reviews?

Are we truly committed to always improving the way we handle our sales efforts? How can we be sure we follow through, converting our commitment to action?

Test Your Knowledge:

Describe generally which members of the team are active in Phase 4.

What does it mean to debrief? Why is it important?

If you lose a deal, how can you save the relationship? Why is it important?

Why should you always improve the process? How can this make your team function more effectively?

Chapter Nine

The Easy Way to Remember the CODE

You made it! You crossed the finish line. I'm proud of you for coming on this journey with me. In this short time, I've given you an extraordinary amount of information and ideas. What you've read has been the by-product of many individuals' effort to share with me the truth about how contractors really work, what their day-to-day sales world looks like, and how it should be structured.

In writing this, I've discovered the strange truth that there really is a numeric code to CODE. If you are a person who easily recalls numbers, here's the one to commit to memory. **4-3-2-8-1.**

---

4   There are four phases to a really solid sales process. Lead generation, lead qualification, the sales pitch and post sales.

3   There are three critical roles that comprise the core skills of the sales team. They are the Prospector, the Technical Expert and the Closer.

2   There are only two types of prospects. The experienced prospect, that has bought your type of product or service before, and the inexperienced prospect, who has never bought your product or service before.

8   There are eight questions that you must try to get answers to in truly qualifying your prospect.

1   There is one goal. Keep the pipeline filled and moving. Yellows to Blues, and Blues to Reds.

Do you know the CODE? Sure you do.

Now get out there and make it work for you!

In conclusion,

A word of sincere thanks....

As I conclude writing this text, I think about the past five years of my life I've committed to intense study of this subject. A lot has happened in five years. I've had two children, and one big baby named CODE. I have no idea how much of my time has really gone into the development of CODE; all I know is that it's been a driving and passionate force, giving my work meaning as I seek to release Rainmakers and entrepreneurs from their plight.

When I pause to consider the sincere kindness and profound faith of my first client, the one who entrusted me with his company's experience and knowledge, I am awestruck. He is the one with Yellow, Blue and Red lenses in his new business visionary glasses. He will always remain in my mind the hero that blazed the learning path for others...and gave the industry the tools to firmly say "no more bids" and mean it.

To my other clients that participated in the national test pilots, you too have contributed so very much to CODE. I would not have been able to write this without you, as you have continued to carry the torch and move CODE forward by refining daily what works and what doesn't. For this, I am truly grateful that you've shared with me your war stories and journey.

To my husband who has stuck with me throughout every challenge we've faced, and has walked with me by faith, I couldn't ask for a more dedicated partner. You have made all of this possible with your support and encouragement. I could never have done this without you.

To my dear friend Susan, your work continues to make mine possible. In life, God provides great journeymen to share the path. Thank you for sharing mine and blessing me so profoundly with your talents.

And to my inspiration and the Chief Dreamer, Michael Gerber. Your life's work has been the pure inspiration for mine. Without you, the critical process driven thinking that supports CODE would not exist. I encountered your unique viewpoint and perspective through *The E-Myth* and have literally never been the same. I am truly blessed to share this journey and time with you, and aspire as you do, to enable the worldwide gift that is Infinite Options.

And to God be the glory.
I asked for something to say...and you entrusted me with CODE. Thanks be to my Lord and Savior, Christ...Who through all things in life can complete His good and perfect work in each of us.

Elizabeth Allen
July 2006

One more perspective from a former client...

Re: CODE / Elizabeth Allen

<u>*Value of CODE*</u>
Our firm has had the pleasure of being introduced to the CODE process by its founder, Elizabeth Allen. For us, CODE is invaluable. The very fundamentals that we all recognize as being critical to our daily business functions, are easily and generally overlooked. CODE has given us a flexible process, tool for documentation, a "to-do" list for follow-up, instilled accountability and created a forum for our core team members to discuss and offer insights and additional information on a potential project/client. Communicate, Organize, Document, Evaluate is essentially everything that CODE has provided. These are the simple things that we should have been doing otherwise and CODE provided an organized process to achieve them. If for not other reason, CODE provided us with a tool to monitor all of the opportunities we are confronted with daily. We have become better at evaluating the probability of a project/client and understanding that not every 'lead' is one that we are suited for. Without CODE, we would still be fumbling around trying to remember what the current status is of a project/client, who's handling the next steps, and constantly backtracking to capture critical information on opportunities.

<u>*Unique Perspective*</u>
Meeting Elizabeth Allen for the first time was truly a pleasure. Elizabeth's professional demeanor, knowledge and non-technical approach is, to say the least exceptional. She brings a very unique measure to the table in that she is not 'design or construction technical' but extremely knowledgeable about the industry as a whole. Her perspective could easily be identified as being one that could easily be that of a client, which is completely invaluable. Elizabeth completely understands the industry and is a true

visionary; "she gets it!" The remarkable value that Elizabeth brings is not just focused on the business development/sales side, she completely understands the challenges faced when marketing professional services. Her ability to bring the marketing element into the mix is extremely useful when either trying to establish your brand or renewing an existing.

As A Speaker
Once you have had the opportunity to listen to Elizabeth Allen present, you come away with a renewed energy. Her upbeat and positive nature is almost contagious. Her method of presenting negatives is always delivered with optimism and options. She can make you stop and really think about what the situation truly is or could be. Elizabeth is engaging and never comes across as being the authority. Her ability to analyze and think things through offers any audience member a refreshing approach and understanding of how important it is to be flexible.

Elizabeth is a powerful and dynamic speaker with a solid sales and marketing background. If you have been to similar sales and marketing presentations, you will appreciate the difference when Elizabeth speaks to you with actual examples of industry-specific experiences to learn and grow from. You will take-away from this presentation valuable tools that you can begin to use immediately to make an impact in your own sales and marketing efforts. I highly recommend Elizabeth as a sales and marketing expert, a very entertaining and engaging speaker, and I am very proud to know her as a colleague and to call her a friend.

-P.C., CPSM, T. Construction

An Update:

A lot has changed in the years since this book was originally written. However, I believe the methods of this book are still extremely relevant today. I've trained and coached many more client companies, using the CODE process and continued to learn approaches that have allowed me to train companies outside of the contracting world.

We've seen the impact on business from a devastating recession. Many businesses, particularly contractors, have lost a lot of business, and many are no longer in business. An observation I've made through this trying time is that, "To the degree you can drive sales, you have job security." Whether you are the principal of a company, a designer, or an apprentice out on the job site, if you bring sales, you have a job.

I've incorporated this observation in my newest book, **Driving Demand: The CODE for Sales.** In today's economy, every business needs everybody to be a prospector. And CODE applies to more than Architects, Engineers, and Construction companies. My latest book is directed at the more general business audience. See the website CODEforSales.com for more information.

With the loss of jobs, I have found myself assisting many people who are unemployed, or "Free Agents," as I prefer to call them. I've found that the CODE process can be turned toward selling yourself as a potential employee or as a new entrepreneur. My observation is that "the only difference between someone who is unemployed and an entrepreneur is that one has decided he or she has something to sell." I teach people how to think like an entrepreneur in my recent book, **The Economy of One: CODE for Free Agents**. See the website Eof1.com for more details.

Along with **The Contractor's CODE for Sales**, I hope you'll find each of my books uniquely helpful. I hope you'll recommend my books to your colleagues and friends. I welcome your feedback at my email address below.

Best wishes to you as you explore and live the world of CODE.

May God truly bless you!

Elizabeth Allen
eallen@codeconstruct.com

ABOUT THE AUTHOR

 Elizabeth Allen is the Principal consultant of the sales consulting firm MarketSmartz, based in Kansas City. A self-employed entrepreneur from the age of 25, she has worked in every facet of strategic market planning, national brand management and executive sales management.

Elizabeth is the creator and developer of CODE®, a proprietary sales and marketing system that has transformed small- and mid-size companies nationwide. In development and test pilots for over ten years, CODE® has transformed the sales process of dozens of companies across the United States. Her sales management systems are the subject of *The Contractor's CODE for Marketing and Sales* (2006) and *Driving Demand: The CODE for Sales: All Hands on Deck* (2014).

Frequently asked to lecture, Elizabeth is a thought leader that delivers cutting edge insight and practical advice on how everyone throughout an organization can meaningfully participate and support the sales process. CODE has been a featured best practice at the national Society of Marketing Professional Services (SMPS) convention in 2006 and has been voted as best practice in numerous national executive peer groups.

During the economic downturn of the Great Recession, Elizabeth devoted much of her time and effort toward helping the many unemployed "Free Agents" transition to a new "Economy of One." From her observation that "the only difference between someone unemployed and an entrepreneur is that one has decided that he or she has something to sell," she developed a new CODE program to teach Free Agents how to "think like an entrepreneur," whether they become an entrepreneur or end up finding a new job. Elizabeth has taught and facilitated this course to a number of Free Agent groups. The program is documented in her ground-breaking book, *The Economy of One: CODE for Free Agents.* (2011)

Elizabeth has served as a facilitator for The Kauffman Foundation's FastTrac program and as a mentor for the KU MBA Graduates Program. She has served as a marketing expert for projects at Sprint, IBM, 3M, & Pfizer and is a founding member of the Kansas City United Way's Women's Leadership Council. She is a recipient of the President's Award from the Kansas City chapter of SMPS and was a featured expert, highlighting industry best practices at the SMPS Los Angeles National Convention in 2006. Her unique expertise and vast experience has been highlighted in InfoWorld, Entrepreneur Magazine, Concrete Monthly, and on a nationally broadcast PBS special. She has been featured in cover stories in the Johnson County (Kansas) Business Times and the Kansas City Small Business Monthly. She is the mother of two children.

Also from Elizabeth Allen:

Most people will have 7 to 10 different jobs by the age of 38, according to a recent study by the Department of Labor.

The
Economy
of One
CODE for Free Agents

Elizabeth Allen

Welcome to the New Normal. Unprepared?

The Economy of One: CODE for Free Agents is designed to help you dramatically improve your value proposition to potential employers and clients. CODE was developed and pioneered over the past 10 years by Elizabeth Allen, a nationally recognized expert in entrepreneurship. Her award-winning work has now been adapted for individuals - those among the millions faced with the unique challenge of reestablishing themselves as viable Free Agents who create their own Economy of One.

What will you learn?

- -A step-by-step process that will help you effectively identify and explore your options. Looking for full-time employment is just one of many paths available to you.
- -Strategic self-promotion, communication and networking skills. You will learn how to engage a straightforward methodology designed to take the guesswork out of the self-promotion "sales" process.
- -Recapture confidence. You will learn 8 critical sets of questions that are deigned to empower you.
- -Insight into the strategic mindset of those doing the hiring. Understand how employer priorities align with yours before you interview.
- -Re-connect to passion, proficiency, and profitability. We will help you identify options that are best suited for your natural abilities and interests.
- -Monitor progress. You will learn how to approach every networking event, job fair or interview with a focused plan.
- -Achieve transparency. Communicate to others your progress so that the question of "what's your plan?" And "what have you been up to?" is easy to address.
- -Go way beyond writing a resume and applying endlessly for every job you see, competing with thousands of others for a job that may not even exist. Instead, engage the market from a very different, targeted approach, utilizing your "personal brand" to get in front of decision-makers.
- -Find support. This program is designed to re-energize you and jump-start your efforts, helping you more effectively engage immediately.

140